I0170363

Aha, The Kingdom Revealed!

-and other stuff

Aha, The Kingdom Revealed!

-and other stuff

Frank Harvey

Copyright Information

Aha, The Kingdom Revealed - and other stuff
By: Frank Harvey

©2020 Frank Harvey
PO Box 810,
Ballina, New South Wales
Australia 2478

Published by:
Good News Fellowship Ministries
220 Sleepy Creek Rd.
Macon, Georgia
ISBN-13: 978-1-7344999-1-9

No part of this book may be reproduced or transmitted in any
form or by any means, electronic or mechanical, including
photocopying, recording, or by an information storage and
retrieval system, without permission in writing from the Author.

Most Scriptures used in this book are from the New King James
Version of the Bible.

'The Holy Bible, New King James Version Copyright ©1982 by
Thomas Nelson, Inc.'
Occasional Scriptures (marked: NLT) are quoted from the New
Living Translation of the Bible:

'Scripture quotations marked NLT are taken from the Holy
Bible, New Living Translation, copyright ©1996, 2004, 2015
by Tyndale House Foundation. Used by permission of Tyndale
House Publishers, Inc., Carol Stream, Illinois 60188.
All rights reserved.'

Please note that the publishing style of this book capitalises
pronouns which refer to the Father, Son and Holy Spirit—and in
this regard will differ from some publisher's style.

Format by : Lisa Walters Buck

Dedication

This book is dedicated to the memory of Dr Wilfred Millington, my late father-in-law and former Dean of the International Bible Training Institute, Burgess Hill, Sussex UK—where I studied and worked for a number of years.

As a student at the I.B.T.I 'Pastor' Millington's lectures on the subject of typology immediately caught my imagination and has remained a life-long fascination for me. The church-world could do with many more teachers of Dr Millington's calibre.

His notes for a book to be published about his teachings were contained in a brief-case, stolen while travelling in the USA shortly before he died. I trust this present book may compensate, in some small measure, for this earlier loss.

Contents

'For the Law (has) a **SHADOW** of good things to come; and **not** the very **image** of the things ...' [Hebrews 10:1]

'Now all these things . . . **are written for our admonition** upon whom the ends of the ages have come.' [I Corinthians 10:11]

Introduction

When I first started writing this book, I was using the working title: 'Types, Shadows – and other stuff.' I was well into the work when I received a new book from insightful bible teacher Adrian Beale. In his book Adrian spurns the use of the term 'types and shadows' in favour of the term: 'Aha, the kingdom revealed!' … and with his kind permission the phrase became part of the final title of my own book.

However, this book will continue to use the term '*types and shadows*', as well as '*other stuff*'- expressions like '*parallelisms*' and '*chiasms*' etc. to explain some literary formats used in the original writing of the scriptures—not in English, but in the language of the people to whom it was first given.

In our generation, the English language is one of the few 'most used' languages spoken around the world; but it is not the original language of the scriptures. And whenever translation is required, some meanings inevitably get lost or blunted in the process.

The English words used are not necessarily incorrect, but they may not convey the meaning, or full impact which the speakers of the original language naturally understood.

For example: how long was it before you learned that the '*eye of a needle*' (Matthew 19:24) referred to an especially low and narrow gate, allowing travellers (but not their loaded camels!) into a city at night after the main gates were closed? It has nothing to do with the eye of a literal sewing needle!

Or, were you ever taught that when the father of the Prodigal ran to meet his son (Luke 15:20) he was making himself a spectacle by lifting his long robe to run and showing his legs—something that a wealthy, important community leader did not do in that culture? When you understand this, you appreciate more than ever the passion of this father to see the restoration of his 'lost' son.

In a thousand other ways the writers of the bible, consciously or unconsciously, were led by the Spirit of God to insert the concept of types, shadows and other literary forms throughout the scriptures. This means that many events are written in a very simplistic or poetic style—but the obvious simplicity of the account allows us to see how the event pre-figures a greater event, perhaps not made obvious for many generations into the future.

An example of this is the story of Abraham and his son Isaac going to Mt Moriah to make a sacrifice. Genesis 22 says Abraham saddled his donkey and chopped the wood for the sacrifice. However, in real life, the donkey is saddled, and the wood is chopped by his servants, because Abraham was a very wealthy man.

This is the 'eastern' way of allowing that Abraham performed these tasks because his command to do so was the primary action which produced the chopped wood and the saddled donkey! Told in this manner, it is easy to pre-figure God the heavenly 'father' arranging for the timber cross upon which the Romans sacrificed His own Son.

By contrast, our 'western' mindset demands that we should be very detailed and very precise. Our account of this story would insist on stating that it was the servants who chopped the wood, etc. We would demand 'credit, where credit is due'! But such detail would rob us of the outstanding Kingdom truths contained within this uncomplicated biblical account.

The Bible tells us the Messiah was, '*slain from the foundation of the world*' (Rev.13:8) and God has chosen us, '*in Him before the foundation of the world.*' (Ephesians 1:4)

Because the coming of Messiah was such a pre-determined part of God's plan for humankind, it is easy to see why the transforming story of Messiah Jesus has been embedded into the structure of the scriptures from the very beginning.

I have written this book to help you, my readers, better understand the concept of 'types and shadows', and several other literary forms which are the structure of the scriptures in their original language.

My hope and prayer are that you will also receive many 'Aha' moments as you encounter further revelation along your Christian pilgrimage of Kingdom discovery.

Enjoy!

Chapter 1

Types – Their Use and Purpose

What is a Type?

Biblical Typology is viewed as a system which uses the **minimum of Words** to express the *maximum of Revelation*!

The study of Biblical Typology—often known as 'types and shadows'—is an attempt to understand how God causes the human mind to understand Eternal and Heavenly matters, by conveying the idea through the use of the word-pictures and illustrations i.e. the many types and shadows we will discuss in this book.

'Types' include those events, people or things which follow the classic pattern of a full-blown Type – (Prototype, Type and Antitype) – while the concept of 'Shadows' embraces types which have no clear prototype. Shadows, therefore, also allow us to speak about such things as Allegories, Metaphors, Proverbs and Parables etc. etc.

> **Minimum of Words . . .**
> **Maximum of**
> **Revelation**

The concept of understanding the Scriptures through this avenue of 'types and shadows' is as old as the Bible itself. Some of the world's most ancient languages are image-based (like Egyptian hieroglyphics), rather than letter-based, as in the English language.

In broad terms, a 'type' refers to a detailed biblical symbol, person, or event which assists the student to uncover the many hidden truths in the Word of God. A 'shadow' however, is a type or symbol which is only a foreshadowing of some future thing or event. It is like the first sketches of an artist or an architect; used by the artisan as a template for the final painting or building.

But sometimes the 'shadows' of the Old Masters are worth almost as much as the finished paintings themselves!

As you read various Bible translations, you will come across words like *examples, similitudes, parables, proverbs, dark sayings, hidden wisdom, figures of speech* etc. Keep your eyes open and you will recognise them throughout the Scriptures, even when the above words may not be mentioned specifically.

The following is a listing of various terminology within the Scriptures which establish this truth (all quoted from NLT):

Job 12:7-8 (in the natural world) 'Just ask the animals, and *they will teach you*. Ask the birds of the sky, and *they will tell you*. Speak to the earth, and *it will instruct you*. Let the fish in the sea *speak to you* ...'

and **John 12:24** '...a kernel of **wheat is planted** in the soil and **dies** ...'

Hosea 12:10 'I sent my prophets to warn you with many *visions and parables*.'

Romans 5:14 'everyone died ... even those who did not disobey an explicit commandment of God, as Adam did. Now Adam is *a symbol, a representation of Christ*, who was yet to come.'

Galatians 4:24 'These two women (Sarah and Hagar) serve as *an illustration* (or *allegory*) of God's two covenants.'

Colossians 2:16-17 'So don't let anyone condemn you for what you eat or drink … For these rules are *only shadows of the reality yet to come*. And Christ himself is that reality.'

Hebrews 7:15 'This change has been made very clear since a different priest, **who is like** (*'likeness'* NKJV) Melchizedek, has appeared.'

Hebrews 9:8-9 'By these regulations the Holy Spirit revealed that the entrance to the Most Holy Place was not freely open as long as the Tabernacle and the system it represented were still in use. This is *an illustration* (*'it was symbolic'* NKJV) pointing to the present time . . .'

Hebrews 10:1 'The old system under the law of Moses was only *a shadow, a dim preview* of the good things to come, not the good things themselves.'

Chapter 2:

The Dress in the Shop Window

A strong 100% Type is usually comprised of three elements; Prototype, Type and Antitype, as contained in the following illustration …

A woman sees a dress in a shop window, the design of which catches her imagination. Arriving home, she uses her dressmaking skills and proceeds to create a paper pattern. From this paper pattern she cuts various pieces of material—sewing them together, until she has copied the dress in the window.

In the concept of biblical typology, **the PROTOTYPE** is the *dress in the window*. It is beautiful in every way—a one-off original, often designed by a Master-craftsman.

The TYPE is like the paper pattern. It is made up of *various pieces*, depending on the complexity of the dress, and when laid side-by-side they are still only a '*shadow*' of the dress in the window—and the paper from which the pattern is made is very *inferior* to the material of the original dress!

The ANTITYPE is the home-made dress, and in the mind of the dressmaker it is *superior to the dress in the window*. It is exactly her fit, made from specially chosen material—and she has probably tweaked it a little to suit her personal sense of design and fashion!

The Prototype is perfect; the Type—the paper pattern—is inferior, but manages to reflect the original design … but the Antitype is Perfect—Plus!

REMEMBER:
A 100% Super-Type is comprised of three elements, as follows:

PROTOTYPE	TYPE/SHADOW	ANTITYPE
A Biblical example:		
Paradise **PAST** (Ezekiel 28)	The **GARDEN OF EDEN** (Gen.1 & 2)	Paradise **FUTURE** (Rev. 21 & 22)

A PROTOTYPE: (*An original image*) is therefore everything that springs from God – and is often understood by looking at the Antitype.

A TYPE: (**Something resembling the original**) is the process between Prototype and Antitype. The word 'Type' is from the Greek '*tupos*' i.e. to leave a mark; to beat by pressure – as in John 20:26 'Unless I see in His hands the *print* of the nails … I will not believe!'

AN ANTITYPE: (*A copy of the original*) bears the image of the Prototype, but not necessarily the Type, because the Type is imperfect. However, it may also be better than the Prototype—*and certainly better than the Type*.

NOTE (a): In Typology a **PROTOTYPE** is not always found!

NOTE (b): A Type is not a moral i.e. when a preacher uses the story of seven times around Jericho to describe seven ways to obtain victory in life, this is an illustration—**it is not a Type!**

Types can be found in (but not limited to) the following Categories

PEOPLE: Adam, Melchizedek, Abraham, Sarah, Isaac, David etc. '… Adam, who is a type of Him who was to come.' (Rom 5:14)

[For a further treatment of OT characters refer to Chapter Nine]

PLACES: Egypt, Jerusalem or Zion, Babylon etc. 'But you have come to Mount Zion and to the city of the living God, the Heavenly Jerusalem …' (Heb. 12:22)

EVENTS: Creation, Noah's Flood and preservation, redemption from Egypt, lifting up the brass serpent, provision of Manna etc. 'Now all these things … were written for our admonition, upon whom the ends of the ages have come.' (1 Cor 10:11)

THINGS: Items such as the Tabernacle furniture, curtains, the laver, the sacrificial lamb, Jordan, Jacob's Ladder etc. '… a new and living way which He consecrated for us, through the veil, that is, His flesh.' (Heb 10:19-20)

INSTITUTIONS: Prophets, Melchizedek's or Aaron's priesthood, Kings, David's kingdom, Tabernacle, Sabbath, Sacrificial systems, Feasts of Israel etc. '… Christ came … with the greater and more perfect tabernacle not made with hands …' (Heb 9:11-12)

Chapter 3:

Types used by New Testament Persons

On the pages of the New Testament we find both Jesus and His Apostles making reference to Old Testament people and buildings in such a way they must be considered to be using pictures or 'types' as the basis of their comments.

For instance, it was **Jesus Himself** who told Nicodemus that the **Serpent on the Pole** (Number 9:8-9) is a 'type' of Salvation for those who look to Christ, (John 3:14) and very importantly, Jesus told the Scribes and Pharisees that **Jonah's experience with the great fish** was a sign of His own coming Resurrection (Matt.12:38-41)—and then added He was *'greater than Solomon'* (Matt.12:42). In this context Jesus notes how the Queen of Sheba came from far away to see King Solomon, in the same way that Gentiles now come to see Jesus.

The **Apostle Peter** tells us that **Noah's Ark**, (Genesis 7/8) which is a type of Salvation, should also be followed by **Water Baptism** (I Peter 3:18—22). In Peter's first sermon on the Day of Pentecost he claimed that **King David was a 'type' of the Christ/Messiah** who was to come.

The **Apostle Paul** also used 'types' in his teaching when, in Romans 5:12-21 for instance, he explains that **Adam is a *'type'*** of Christ—and in his I Corinthians 15 discourse on Resurrection he contrasts the negative results of Adam's disobedience with the positive results of Christ's obedience and Resurrection: '**The first man Adam became a living being. The last Adam became a life-giving spirit**.' (I Corinthians 15:45)

The **writer of the book of Hebrews** frequently uses 'types' throughout the book—so many, that you will find them listed in detail in **APPENDIX E**.

Some Types are very Obvious

KING DAVID is one of the clearest 'types' of Christ, because the coming Redeemer is called 'David' in the book of Ezekiel (Ezekiel 34:23-24; 37:24-25)

David was a mighty warrior King.	Jesus is the mighty warrior King.
David was a shepherd/King who ruled over God's people in faithfulness.	Jesus is the Good Shepherd and the King of Kings who rules over God's people in perfect covenantal faithfulness.
David faced off against the enemy of God's people and defeated him with his own weapon.	Jesus faced off against the ultimate enemy of God and His people and defeated him with his own weapon.
David was a type of Christ in that he entered into a battle of representative warfare.	Jesus faced off against the ultimate enemy of God as a representative of the forces of righteousness.
David had a band of 'mighty men' who were with him in his sufferings.	Jesus had a band of disciples who were with Him through the period of His humiliation and suffering.
David's mighty men were with him when he ate the showbread in the Tabernacle.	Jesus' disciples were with Him when they walked through the grain fields on the Sabbath (Matt. 12:1-8).
David had a betrayer who—when his plot was uncovered—went and hanged himself.	Jesus had a betrayer who—when his plot was uncovered—went and hanged himself.
David crossed over the Brook Kidron when he was betrayed by Ahithophel.	Jesus crossed over the Brook Kidron when He was betrayed by Judas.

A Further Basic Illustration of a Type

TYPE:	ANTITYPE:
GENESIS – Tree of Life	REVELATION – Tree of Life
(Refer Genesis 1-3 and Revelation 4-5 & 21-22)	

A GARDEN in Eden	A CITY in Heaven
ONE Tree in Eden . . .	MANY trees in Heaven
With **restricted approach** to tree in Eden	NONE in Heaven
Adam walked/talked with God in the evening – **limited Fellowship**	NO limit in Heaven - God Dwells Eternally in the midst of the Sons of God
Possibility of SIN in Eden	NONE in Heaven – Believers are the Sons of God
Obedience – **with a free-will that could sin**	Obedience – **with a free-will of the Divine Nature**

Some Rules for Interpretation

1) Always be sure of your antitypical scripture reference.

2) Understand the Type clearly, so as to understand the Antitype clearly.

3) Interpret the Type in the light of fundamental truths.

4) When working with a 'shadow' make sure you have at least two or three scriptures to support your interpretation.

NOTE: There is always more in the Antitype, in as much as it takes all the types of Joseph, Abraham, Moses and Aaron etc. to make the Antitype of Christ.

The TYPE is discerned through the ANTITYPE, as in the following example:

THE PASCHAL LAMB (Exodus12)	THE LAMB OF GOD (John.1:29/30)

TYPE	ANTITYPE
Taken from other lambs	Jesus was a man & stood with the crowd on the Banks of Jordon – until revealed to John the Baptist.
Examination of the lamb	Initial testing in the Wilderness
3-1/2 days for examination – then killed	Followed for 3-1/2 years scrutiny by Scribes & Pharisees – then killed
Flesh then eaten - loins girded - freed from Bondage	The Christian experience of 'life in Christ' – looking for Him.
Paschal for a Nation	The Lamb of God for the World

Note: A Sacrament is not a Type – it only prefigures something

We end this chapter by taking a quick look at Psalm 22.

This Psalm is well-recognised as a Prophetic insight into the suffering of Jesus Christ, when dying as the Messiah and Saviour of the world. It is also believed that Jesus would have quoted this Psalm, as a prayer, while hanging on the Cross.

NEW TESTAMENT	PSALM 22 (& others)
Matt. 27:38 – 'Then two robbers were crucified with Him …'	vs.16/17 – 'They pierced My hands and My feet …'
Matt. 27:45 – 'About the 9th hour Jesus cried out …' Eli, Eli, lama sabachthani?' …'	vs. 1 – 'My God, My God, why have You forsaken Me?'
Matt. 27:41 – 'The Chief priests ... mocking (said) He saved others: Himself He cannot save …'	vs. 7 – 'All those who see Me ridicule Me … saying …
Matt 27:43 – 'He trusted in God; let Him deliver Him now.'	vs. 7 – … He trusted in the Lord, let Him rescue Him.'
John 19:23/24 – 'the soldiers … took … His tunic … they said therefore, Let us … cast lots for it.'	vs.18 – 'They divide My garments among them, and for My clothing they cast lots.'
Matt. 27:48 – (Filled) 'a sponge … with sour wine … and offered it to Him to drink.'	Ps. 69:21 – 'For my thirst they gave me vinegar to drink.'
John 19:31/32 – 'Then the soldiers came and broke the legs of the (those) crucified with Him, But when they … saw that He was already dead, they did not break His legs …'	Ps. 34:19/20 – 'Many are the afflictions of the righteous, but the Lord delivers him … He guards all his bones; Not one of them is broken.'
John 19:34 – 'But one of the soldiers pierced His side with a spear, and immediately blood and water came out.'	Zech. 12:10 – 'They shall look on Me whom they pierced.'

Chapter 4:

Further Notes on the Purpose of Types

There is often a Moral Example in the Old Testament actions and events.

Remember: A 'type' is not a moral; but from the various actions and events which can be considered as 'types', there are definite moral examples to be drawn.

AN EXAMPLE: is the general history of the Children of Israel, as described in I Corinthians 10:1-13

> 'These things (*the history of Israel*) happened to them as examples for us.
> They were written down to warn us who live at the end of the age.'
> (I Corinthians 10:11 NLT)

• **The Divine Contents in the facts, as they are recorded, reveal the plans of God throughout the Ages.**

If you or I were to record these same actions/events we would undoubtedly include numerous details not found in the Bible. It is these additional details which would cloud the issue and obscure the typological value in the event.

AN EXAMPLE: Refer Genesis chapters 22/24—where Abraham (as a 'type' of God the Father) prepares to sacrifice his only son Isaac (as a 'type' of Christ)—and Isaac (as 'type' of Christ) welcomes the arrival of his Bride Rebekah (as a 'type' of the Church).

Take note of:

- **The activity of Abraham:** He **i)** saddled his Ass, and **ii)** chopped the wood. This was unusual. What were servants for? But if the servants did actually complete these tasks, it is so recorded in the Scriptures that the ***original command of Abraham*** takes precedence over the action of the servants.

- **Abraham and Isaac climbed the mountain together**, indicating the ***faith*** of Abraham (the father) and the ***willingness*** of Isaac (the son) in this act of sacrificial worship.

- There is **no specific mention made of Isaac returning down the mountain with his father**. This is a 'type' of Christ returning to Heaven after the Resurrection and no longer being seen on the earth, until … Isaac (as a 'type' of Christ) is next mentioned in Genesis 24:62-64 when he sees the Unnamed servant bringing Rebekah (his wife-to-be) to him.

- **The Birth of Rebekah, the Bride of Isaac:** The mention of Rebekah's birth is made immediately after the '*Resurrection*' of Isaac—in the same way that the Church, 'the Bride of Christ' was born out of the wounded side of the crucified Christ.

> 'Abraham reasoned that if Isaac died, God was able to bring him back to life again. And in a sense, Abraham did receive his son back from the dead.' (Hebrews 11:19 NLT)

- **There is a foundational concept of the New Testament 'church' hidden in Old Testament events.** These 'types' are not necessarily a 'simplification' of truth; but rather a starting point and a word-picture of divine truth.

Remember: The awesomeness of divine realities can only be absorbed by our human brains in the form of word-pictures.

Refer Ezekiel 1:28 NLT – 'All around him was a glowing halo, like a rainbow shining in the clouds on a rainy day. This is what the glory of the Lord looked like to me. When I saw it, I fell face down on the ground . . .'

AN EXAMPLE: Refer Genesis chapter 24 – **Rebekah becomes the Bride of Isaac.**

The SEARCH FOR A BRIDE FOR ISAAC	
NEW TESTAMENT TRUTH	**OLD TESTAMENT ACTIVITY**
Ministry of the Holy Spirit	Revealed in the activity of the Unnamed Servant, seeking a Bride for Isaac
Spiritual Gifts	Shadowed in the *Gifts given to Rebekah from Isaac, by the hand of the Unnamed Servant.
*The servant travelled with ten camels. Assuming he rode one of them himself, nine others were available to carry gifts for Rebekah. This becomes a 'type' of the Nine Gifts of the Spirit as detailed in 1 Corinthians 12:7-11	
The Bride of Christ	Rebekah, the Bride of Isaac

All of the above Examples are outstanding New Testament Truths, which are without precedent – except in the Types and Shadows of the Old Testament Scriptures.

Chapter 5:

Typology and the Holy Spirit

As you study the topic of Typology you will soon observe that Jesus Christ is the main thrust of types and shadows.

However, we should always be on the lookout for the ministry and activity of the Holy Spirit in the Old Testament scriptures.

The Holy Spirit is the only person of the Godhead/Trinity to not have a personal name, and He is often described as the Unseen member of the Trinity. Since earliest times theologians have seen the work of the unnamed Servant in the Isaac and Rebekah story (Genesis 22 & 24) as a symbolic 'type' of God the Holy Spirit, operating in the Old Testament, thus:

Abraham — **God the Father**
Isaac — **Jesus the Son**
Isaac carried the wood up Mt Moriah
   — as Jesus carried the wood of His cross.

Isaac is figuratively 'resurrected' from death — as a ram 'caught in the thicket' is provided in his place.

The Ram — **its horns caught in the thicket is symbolic of Christ the Son of God** surrendering His divine authority to become the humble Son of Man

*Unnamed Servant seeking a Bride for Isaac
              – Holy Spirit
Rebecca   **– The Church, the 'Bride of Christ'**

*Although unnamed in this story, it is widely accepted by Rabbinic scholars that he was Abraham's steward Eliezer, whose name by Divine coincidence means: 'Helper'!

> 'And I will pray the Father, and He will give you another Helper, that He may abide with you forever—the Spirit of truth ...' (John 14:16/17)

The Holy Spirit is pictured/shadowed in the activity of the Dove sent out from Noah's Ark:

THE MINISTRY OF THE HOLY SPIRIT

THE DOVE is the only clean creature in the world
a. Without a Gall – therefore no poison in its system

b. Gentle in its manner – **'harmless as doves'** (Matt.10:16)

c. A constant lover – Romans 5:5 (**'the love of God has been poured out in our hearts by the Holy Spirit.'**)

NOAH'S DOVE is a Dispensational 'type'/Picture

First Flight	Spasmodic visits of the Holy Spirit in the Old Testament. No permanent dwelling place.
Second Flight	Returns seven days later (a perfect cycle) Significance of No: 7 = Completeness.
The Dove brought back an Olive Branch, as the 'first fruit' of a new creation. This is a 'type' of the Holy Spirit coming on Christ—and taking Him to Glory in the Ascension.	
Third Flight	The Dove never returned i.e. the Holy Spirit coming to take up His permanent residence in the New Testament Church.

The Holy Spirit is pictured/shadowed in the Consecration of Aaron and his sons:

Another 'type' of the Holy Spirit's work in the life of Jesus and all believers exists in a comparison between the Anointing of Aaron and the Anointing of his sons. Note how **varying amounts of the same oil** was used in the consecration of Aaron and his sons.

Leviticus 8:12 reports that Moses **poured oil on Aaron's head** …described in Psalm 133:2 as 'running down on the beard – and running down on the edge of his garments…'

In contrast to this, Leviticus 8:12 reports that Moses only **'took some of the anointing oil' and sprinkled** Aaron's sons. [Refer Chart towards the end of Chapter Seven]

The Pillars of Cloud and Fire are 'types' of New Testament Baptisms

During their time in the Wilderness, the people of God were guided by the presence of God, in the form of the pillar of cloud by day, and the pillar of fire by night. (Exodus 13:21; Numbers 9:15-23).

The Apostle Paul teaches us:

> 'Moreover, brethren, I do not want you to be unaware that all our fathers were under the cloud, all passed through the sea, all were baptized into Moses in the cloud and in the sea …' (1 Corinthians 10:1-2).

Paul is using the wilderness story as 'types' of baptisms the New Testament believer must experience.

Israel was not only 'baptised' in the Red Sea ('type' of the blood of Christ), but also in the cloud, the Shekinah glory of God ('type' of the Baptism in the Holy Spirit). At Pentecost tongues of fire rested on the '120' as the outward evidence of the Baptism in the Holy Spirit. (Acts 2:3)

> 'When he, the Spirit of truth, has come, He will guide you into all truth ...' (John 16:13).

In the Gospels there are a number of events involving an Unnamed person, who can be accepted as a 'type' of the Holy Spirit and His activity.

The Unnamed Woman of Luke 15:8-10

The Luke 15 account of a shepherd who goes searching for a lost sheep is a beautiful 'type' of Jesus, the Son of God. The account of the father who welcomes the return of his lost son is, similarly, a type of God the Father ... and the account of the woman searching for her lost coin is a fitting type of the work of the Holy Spirit. In this story the woman searches for her coin with a light and a broom—her broom being a picture of the Holy Spirit in his 'sweeping' and cleansing work; and the light as a type of the Spirit's enlightening work. *'However, when He, the Spirit of truth, has come, He will guide you into all truth ... and He will tell you things to come.'* (John 16:13)

The Unnamed Innkeeper in Luke 10:35

The 'Good Samaritan' is obviously a picture of Jesus showing mercy to the man who was robbed and injured by thieves. After attending to this man's immediate needs ('bandaged his wounds, pouring on oil and wine), the Samaritan takes him to an Inn (type of a local church as a Hospice!), to be further cared for by the Innkeeper (the Holy Spirit?).

The Unnamed Servant in Luke 14:16-24

This servant asks men to come to the *'great supper'* — a picture of the gospel feast. The servant invites people, and then 'compels them to come in'. Certainly, a good picture of the work of the Holy Spirit in bringing people to Salvation through the preaching of the Gospel.

The Unnamed Man Bearing a Pitcher in Luke 22:7-13

When preparing for the Passover, Jesus directed His disciples to enter the city, where '***a man will meet you carrying a pitcher of water; follow him into the house which he enters.***' This is a 'type' of the Holy Spirit's activity in using the Scriptures ('a pitcher of water') to lead and guide us.

The Unnamed Doorkeeper in John 10:1-6

As the Good Shepherd approaches the door of the sheepfold the Doorkeeper opens it to him, because he recognises him as the genuine owner of sheep under his care (*rather than sheep-stealers, who climb over the wall!*). As a 'type' the Doorkeeper's recognition of the Good Shepherd demonstrates the intimate relationship between Jesus Christ and the Holy Spirit—both having a role in caring for the sheep.

Chapter 6:

The Tabernacle — Construction & Placement

Exodus chapters 23-40 and Hebrews chapters 9-10

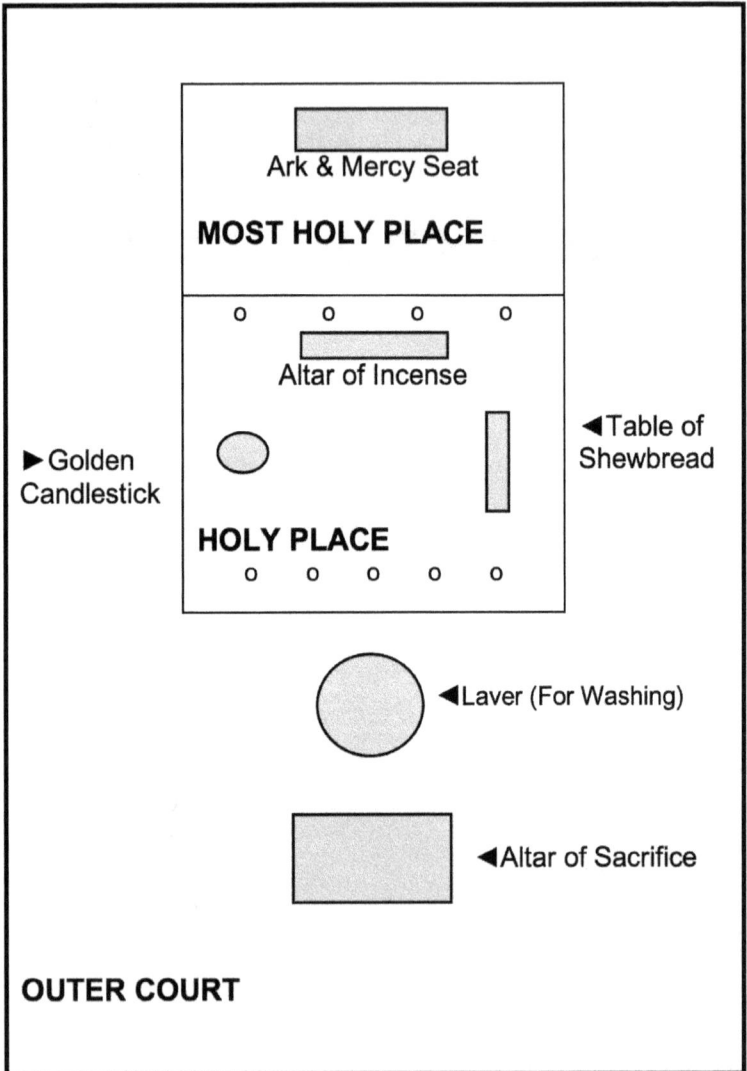

Ark & Mercy Seat

MOST HOLY PLACE

o   o   o   o

Altar of Incense

◀Table of Shewbread

▶Golden Candlestick

HOLY PLACE

o   o   o   o   o

◀Laver (For Washing)

◀Altar of Sacrifice

OUTER COURT

What was the Tabernacle all about?

When Moses went up into the mountain for forty days and nights to meet with God (Exodus 25:8-9), he was given a glimpse into the function and processes of the heavenly Kingdom. Rather than being a randomly designed structure, the design of the Tabernacle was given to him by God, to represent what Moses had seen in the heavenlies—with the added instruction that he was not to deviate in any way from the plan.

> 'Have the people of Israel build me a holy sanctuary so I can live among them. You must build this Tabernacle and its furnishings exactly according to the pattern I will show you ... (and) ... be sure that you make everything according to the pattern I have shown you here on the mountain.' (Exodus 25:8-9 & 40 NLT)

We must clearly understand it was God's intention, from way back in Eternity Past, that Christ would suffer a substitutionary death at the hands of mankind; be resurrected from the dead; ascend back to the Father and be glorified. The accomplishment of Salvation through the Cross of Christ allows

> Slogan-ed on the walls of Heaven!

heaven to become the eternal home of those who place their faith in Him. So real was this intention that Heaven treated it as if it had already happened. It was like it was 'slogan-ed' on all the walls of heaven!

This being the case, Moses saw heaven already containing the full results of Salvation, and what he saw was also incorporated into the design plans of the Tabernacle which God gave him.

Hebrews 3:5 NLT says of the Tabernacle built by Moses that *'His work was an illustration of the truths God would reveal later.'*

The construction of the Tabernacle; its priesthood, animal sacrifices and the national feast days of Israel are all encoded with the story of the Cross of Calvary. It is the task of the diligent student to learn to decode as much of this design as he can.

The Tabernacle system of animal sacrifice was God's way of re-establishing the lost concept of coming into the true Presence of God by way of sacrifice.

What a pity the writer of the book of Hebrews did not have the time to 'explain these things in detail now'! (Hebrews 9:5 NLT) ... and how sad to read his earlier comments in chapter five:

> 'There is much more we would like to say about this, but it is difficult to explain, especially since you are spiritually dull and don't seem to listen. You have been believers so long now that you ought to be teaching others. Instead, you need someone to teach you again the basic things about God's word.' (Hebrews 5:11-12 NLT)

The next two chapters will cover only some of the basic 'types' found in the Tabernacle and its associated activities.

Types Portrayed in the Tabernacle

There are an amazing number of 'types' located in the details of the Tabernacle, and the book of Hebrews makes frequent reference to them.

PROTOTYPE	TYPE	ANTITYPE
Heavenly worship of God which occurred in Ages past . . .	The Tabernacle built by Moses	The heavenly 'Tabernacle' – in the future Kingdom of God.
. . . of which Moses' Tabernacle was only a copy: '**Be sure that you make everything according to the pattern I have shown you here on the mountain.**' Exodus 25:40 & Hebrews 8:5 NLT		▼ ▼ ▼ ▼ ▼
	'(*Jesus*) ministers in the heavenly Tabernacle, the true place of worship that was built by the Lord and not by human hands.' (Hebrews 8:2 NLT)	
Refer also: 'They serve in a system that is only a copy, a shadow of the real one in heaven.' (Hebrews 8:5 NLT) 'With His own blood—not the blood of bulls and goats—He entered the Most Holy Place once for all time and secured our redemption forever.' (Hebrews 9:12 NLT) '... and, so ... we can boldly enter heaven's Most Holy Place because of the blood of Jesus.' (Hebrews 10:19 NLT)		

Note: While the Tabernacle as a whole is a 'type' of the process of Worship, the Most Holy Place i.e. the innermost 'Tent' is a 'type' of Christ and His ministry.

Why Bother to Study the Tabernacle?

- The details of the Tabernacle, its priesthood, offerings and construction occupy thirteen chapters of the book of Exodus (Chaps.24-31 & 35-40). This is the 'elephant in the room' of Exodus—and must not be ignored!

- The Tabernacle is a picture-lesson of God's redemptive program, as progressively revealed throughout scripture; together with an understanding of how Christ fulfilled this Plan.

- An understanding of the Tabernacle assists our understanding of much of the book of Hebrews, as well as many other New Testament scriptures.

- The function of the Old Testament priesthood is a picture-story of Christ's priestly ministry—as well as the New Testament believer's own priestly role before God.

- An understanding of the sacrifices of the Tabernacle teach us about the need for a blood sacrifice for sin; for 'without the shedding of blood there is no forgiveness.' (Hebrews 9:22 NLT)

- Bishop T. D. Jakes (Potters House USA) has described the Tabernacle as being 'The Gospel in a Tent!'

The General Layout

Note: The Tabernacle Plans which are given to Moses commence, from the inside of the structure, with the construction of the Ark of the Testimony (Exodus 24:10+) ... through to the making of the curtains of the Outer Courtyard (Exodus 38:9+) ... and concluding with the making of the priestly garments (Exodus 39:1+) ... and the final erection of the Tabernacle (Exodus 40:1+).

'Then the cloud covered the tabernacle of meeting, and the glory of the Lord filled the tabernacle. And Moses was not able to enter the tabernacle of meeting, because the cloud rested above it, and the glory of the Lord filled the tabernacle.

Whenever the cloud was taken up from above the tabernacle, the children of Israel would go onward in all their journeys ... For the cloud of the Lord was above the tabernacle by day, and fire was over it by night, in the sight of all the house of Israel, throughout all their journeys.' (Exodus 40:34-38)

[Refer Appendix A for a full listing of the materials used in the construction of the Tabernacle.]

Source: By Ruk7 - Own work, CC BY-SA 3.0
https://upload.wikimedia.org/wikipedia/commons/1/18/Stiftshuette_Modell_Timnapark.jpg

MATERIALS USED IN TABERNACLE (Exodus 25:3-7)

MATERIAL - TYPOLOGICAL MEANING

GOLD - Deity

SILVER - Redemption

BRONZE/BRASS - Strength or Judgment

BLUE - Heaven

PURPLE - Kingship/Royalty

SCARLET Thread - Earthly Glory and Blood of Christ

LINEN - Holiness & Purity

GOAT'S HAIR - Sin Offering

RAM SKINS - Judgment & Substitution

GOAT SKINS - Sacrifice for Sin

ACACIA WOOD - Incorruptible Humanity

HOOKS - Pilgrimage & Transiency

OLIVE OIL for Lamps - Anointing of the Spirit

SPICES - for the anointing oil & the fragrant incense, as a sweet-smelling fragrance to God.

ONYX STONES for the Ephod and **GEMSTONES** to be set in the priest's Breast-plate

- Value, Beauty and Durability.

Significance of the Tabernacle

a) It indicated God's desire to share our human experience

b) It taught a sublime monotheism – i.e. 'one God'.

c) It taught the spirituality/reality of God (but note: there were NO images!)

d) The Holiness of God was emphasised

e) It taught the dual aspect of the Ministry of Israel to the world … i) to serve Man – ii) to serve God.

This dual ministry in seen in the Furnishings of the Holy Place:

Altar of Incense	- to pray
Candlestick	- to illuminate
Table of Shewbread	- to feed hungry souls

Tabernacle Construction –
The Holy and Most Holy Places

These two sections of the Tabernacle were constructed with a number of upright boards made from Acacia wood. Each board had two tenons, which were set into silver wedges at the base and strengthened by rings holding the boards at the four corners. The whole structure was then further strengthened by a series of parallel wooden bars, also made from Acacia wood, attached to the boards through rings. Both rings and bars were overlaid in gold. (Exodus 36:20)

Tabernacle Construction – Outer Coverings

The roofing of this tent-like structure was finally constructed with four different coverings.

The FIRST COVERING was only visible from the inside, seen by the priests as they ministered in the Holy Place and the Most Holy Place. These were woven from fine twisted **LINEN**, decorated with Cherubim (the Guardians of God's holiness) and using the colours: purple, scarlet and blue.

These colours are 'types' of the various roles of Jesus, as also expressed in the obvious themes of the four Gospels

COLOUR:	STATUS:	GOSPEL:
PURPLE	The King	**Matthew**
SCARLET	The Servant	**Mark**
WHITE (Linen)	The Son of Man	**Luke**
BLUE	The Son of God	**John**

The **SECOND COVERING** was made of woven goat's **HAIR**, which represents the blackness of mankind's sin. The goat was an animal of sacrifice (Leviticus 16:5) and this first covering is a 'type' of Christ, whose sacrifice covers us, so that God does not see our past sins when we hide in Christ's death for us. (Goats were only used for a sin offering – Leviticus 16:5)

The **THIRD COVERING** was created from Ram's **SKINS** dyed Red, which is a 'type' of Christ's blood covering the sins of the world.

The **FINAL OUTER COVERING** was again created from **SKINS** – perhaps Badger or Porpoise or 'fine Goatskin leather' (NLT). The text is somewhat unclear, but they would be unattractive and weatherproof. This covering is a 'type' of Christ, in that His physical appearance was very ordinary, and the world saw 'nothing beautiful or majestic about his appearance, nothing to attract us to him …' (Isaiah 53:2/3). The beauty of the Tabernacle was seen only on the inside, after entering correctly through the Door—so also is the excellence of Christ discovered in this way.

There was only one Entrance Gate into the Tabernacle

Christ is the only gate into the presence of God. 'I am the door' (John 10:7) and 'having boldness to enter the Holiest by the blood of Jesus …' (Hebrews 10:19).

[Note: this Entrance faced East – eliminating worship of the Sun!]

The Tabernacle – in the Middle of the Twelve Tribes

When it was time to strike-camp and move out, the various parts of the Tabernacle and furnishings were carried among the twelve tribes.

With the sounding of silver trumpets and the waving of tribal banners the tribes made a great sight as they marched out toward their next encampment.

The **Ark of the Covenant** ('type' of the Presence of God) led the way—carried by the **Levites**.

The Tribe of **JUDAH**, together with **Issachar and Zebulun** (camped on the **East**) came next.

They were followed by **REUBEN**, together with **Simeon and Gad** (camped on the **South**)

Next came **EPHRAIM**, together with **Manasseh and Benjamin** (camped on the **West**).

Finally, acting as a rear-guard was **DAN**, together with **Asher and Naphtali** (camped on the **North**). Full details of which tribe carried which part of the Tabernacle, and the names of their tribal leaders are located in Number 10:11-27.

If you make your own chart of where these tribes were camped, it is possible to view their position forming the shape of the Cross, with the Tabernacle in the heart of the design.

Other commentators also see the layout of the Tabernacle furnishings as representing the shape of the Cross. For some, this may be no more than just a helpful way of remembering the layout!

Chapter 7:

The Tabernacle
– Furnishings & Priesthood

The Types in the Tabernacle Furnishings
Refer Exodus 36-40

In this section we continue our listing of the 'types' lo-cated in the Tabernacle – taking a further look at the Tabernacle and its furnishings.

The key to understanding the Tabernacle is Christ Himself. The Tabernacle, and later the Temple, typified the places and the manner in which God met with His people and dealt with their sins, after they were freed from Egyptian bondage.

They were a type of the yet-to-be-born (Incarnate) Christ and His ministry on behalf of men and women (John 1:14). The priesthood itself was a 'type' of the one and only perfect priest, the Lord Jesus Christ.

In a similar manner, the various Offerings, Feasts, and Ceremonies are 'types' of various aspects of Redemption through the Messiah; as well as the life and life-style of the redeemed.

The Old Testament characters are a 'type' of the New Testament people of faith, and the locations of Old Testament events are often 'types' of spiritual places and conditions of the Christian life and experience.

The Outer Courtyard of the Tabernacle contained the Brazen Altar and the Bronze Laver:

a) **The Brazen Altar** was the first piece of furniture encountered as you entered the Courtyard of the Tabernacle. It was large and unavoidable and it is a 'type' of Christ's sacrifice, without which there is no further entry into the Presence of God. 'Behold! The Lamb of God who takes away the sin of the world!' (John 1:29)

b) **The Bronze Laver** (was a wash-basin made from polished brass mirrors). This is a 'type' of Christ as the Word of God, who has the ability to both show us our faults (as looking in mirror) and also bring cleansing from those faults. '… that (Christ) might sanctify and cleanse the (Church) with the washing of water by the word …' (Eph. 5:26) 'God is light … and if we walk in the light as He is in the light … the blood of Jesus Christ His Son cleanses us from all sin.' (I John I:5-9)

[**Note:** The Outer Courtyard was lit by natural light. It was a totally natural place.]

The Inner Courtyard (or Holy Place) of the Tabernacle
was the first room entered by the Priest and it contained three pieces of furniture i.e. the Table of Presence (or Shewbread), the Menorah or Golden Lampstand and the Altar of Incense.

a) **The Table of Shewbread** (or 'bread-of-face') is a 'type' of Christ, who is the spiritual life sustainer of every Christian believer. 'I am the bread of life. He who comes to Me shall never hunger …' (John 6:35)

The twelve loaves of bread on the table were changed every seven days, but were left undisturbed when Israel was on the march, which is a 'type' of the undisturbed unity of God's people. The table was covered with a scarlet cloth, speaking of the blood of Christ; and the bread was eaten by the priests at the change-over time, being symbolic of fellowship, reconciliation and communion.

b) **The Altar of Incense** was the place of 'a perpetual incense before the Lord'. (Exodus 30:1-10).

This Altar is a reminder that Christ is always making intercession for us (Jn. 17; Heb. 7:25; Rev. 8:3-5). It also symbolizes the worship of the believer (Jn. 4:21/24); and is a reminder that the prayers of believers are never forgotten! (Rev. 8:3, 4; Ps. 141:2; 1 Tim. 2:1-5).

c) **The Menorah or Lampstand of Pure Gold** was the only source of light in the Holy Place. *For a full treatment of the Menorah refer Chapter Eight.*

[**Note:** The Inner Courtyard had no windows and was lit by the 24/7 light from the seven flames of the Golden Lampstand. It was a part-natural and part-spiritual place.]

The Most Holy Place of the Tabernacle contained the Ark of the Covenant, the Mercy Seat and the Shekinah Glory (Light) of God:

This Most Holy Place was entered by the High Priest, only one day of the year on Yom Kippur, the Day of Atonement.

It represented God's dwelling place among men (Heb. 9:24). However, it can also be understood as a 'type' of the physical body of Jesus (Jn. 2:19-21); and it is not unlike the local church (1 Cor. 3:16-17; 6:19) or the universal church consisting of all believers in Christ (Ephesians 2:21).

a) **The Ark of the Covenant** (Exodus 25:10-16) contained the Law, a jar of Manna and Aaron's budded Rod. It was a timber box, totally covered in gold both inside and outside, which is an obvious 'type' of Christ Himself—the God-Man i.e. 'Gold-Timber'.

Christ was able to fulfil the Law because He was sin-less (Matt. 5:17, 18); the Manna is a 'type' of Christ the Bread of Life; and Aaron's budded Rod is a 'type' of the Resurrection ability of God. ***Just as the Ark of the Covenant contained God's witness to Israel, Christ is God's witness to mankind.***

b) **The Mercy Seat** was the gold lid or cover on top of the Ark of the Covenant (Exodus 25:17-21; Lev. 16:13-16). The Mercy Seat is the cover, the covering or removal of sin by means of expiatory sacrifice. It is the Old Testament throne of grace. Justice and mercy met there, and the blood of the innocent sacrifice covers the sin of Israel. Christ is that covering for sin for the whole world (Heb. 9:5 and 1 Jn. 2:2). He is the Mercy Seat.

> 'For everyone has sinned; we all fall short of God's glorious standard. Yet God, in his grace, freely makes us right in his sight. He did this through Christ Jesus when he freed us from the penalty of our sins. For God presented Jesus as the sacrifice for sin. People are made right with God when they believe that Jesus sacrificed his life, shedding his blood. This sacrifice shows that God was being fair when he held back and did not punish those who sinned in times past. For he was looking ahead and including them in what he would do in this present time ...' (Romans 3:23-26 NLT)

c) **The Shekinah Glory was certainly not a 'furnishing' – but it was the heavenly light in the Most Holy Place (a place with no window to the outside light.)**

'Glory' can be described as the self-manifestation of God or His manifested presence with men (Refer: Exodus 14:19; 33:18-20; 34:5-7 and 40:34).

The Most Holy Place filled with the Shekinah Glory is a 'type' of God's dwelling place in heaven (Hebrews 9:24).

God, as represented by the Cherubim, is pictured as looking down upon the Mercy Seat; as well as acting as a Guide to the Israelites while in the Wilderness.

'Then the cloud covered the Tabernacle, and the glory of the Lord filled the Tabernacle. Moses could no longer enter the Tabernacle because the cloud had settled down over it, and the glory of the Lord filled the Tabernacle.' (Exodus 40:34/35 NLT)

[**Note**: The Most Holy Place had no windows and was lit by the light of the Shekinah Glory of God. It was a totally supernatural place.]

Between these two 'Holy Places' was stretched a curtain, which became known as the 'veil' in the Tabernacle (and later in the Temple).

This veil (Exodus 26:31-35) is an outstanding 'type' of Christ's own body, through which we come freely into God's Presence. (Heb. 10:20; Matt. 27:51). The act of crucifixion ripped apart the body of Christ, but as an immediate result of His death, it is recorded in Matthew 27:51 that '… behold, the veil of the temple was torn in two from top to bottom.'

Jewish records indicate the veil in the Tabernacle was 10cm (4 inches) thick – and in the Temple it may have been as much as 30cm (12 inches) thick, so it was not possible for a human hand to rip it apart in this way. Ripping it open was a heavenly action, and proclaimed that the way into the most intimate presence of God was now made available for all people—not just for one single High Priest, once each year!

The Nature of Priesthood (Hebrews 7:23 – 8:2)

The High Priest was set apart by God to offer the yearly Atonement for the Nation. Jesus was God's High Priest who offered Himself as the perfect sacrifice for our sins.

- Human priests have weaknesses and infirmity (Hebrews 7:29)

- They must sacrifice daily for their own sins (Hebrews 7:27)

- There is a constant repetition of sacrifices (Hebrews 10:11)

- They are Appointed without an Oath – on the basis of casual commandment

- They could not continue by reason of death (Hebrews 7:23)

- The Levitical Priesthood was destined to be superseded

> 'Therefore, if perfection were through the Levitical priesthood ... what further need was there that another priest should rise according to the order of Melchizedek, and not be called according to the order of Aaron? ... there were many priests, because they were prevented by death from continuing. But He, because He continues forever, has an unchangeable priesthood. Therefore, He is also able to save to the uttermost those who come to God through Him, since He always lives to make intercession for them.' (Extracted from Hebrews 7:11-25)

Aaron was a Type of Christ

The first High Priest Aaron and his sons are a type of believers in Christ who, with Christ, constitute the royal and priestly family of which Christ is the Head.

Israel acted in and through Aaron – but Believers come to God through Christ.

The Anointing
(Refer Exodus chapter 29 and Leviticus chapter 8)

In the consecration of Aaron and his sons there is a Type of the Anointing of the Holy Spirit on Believers.	
AARON and his sons	**JESUS and His believers**
AARON anointed with a 'great' quantity of Oil	JESUS CHRIST received the Holy Spirit 'without measure'
(Refer Psalm 133 – Lev. 8:12)	
This was followed by a Sacrifice	Then Christ made His great Sacrifice
Aaron's sons took part in and of this Sacrifice	A Believer must first share in the Sacrifice of Christ . . .
Then they were anointed with a 'smaller' quantity of Oil.	. . . then the Believers can be Baptised in the Holy Spirit
(Note: They were also sprinkled with the blood of the sacrifice as well as the Anointing Oil)	

The High Priest and his Breastplate

After putting on his Holy Garments the High Priest attached a Chest-piece or Breastplate, positioned over his heart, which was adorned with twelve Gemstones. The names of the Twelve Tribes were engraved on them (although we are not told their order). The exact modern equivalent for these stones is also unknown, but those which appear below are named by the New Living Translation (together with their approximate colour).

This meant that whenever the High Priest went into the Tabernacle and/or Presence of God he took with him the twelve gemstones over his heart (which represented all of Israel)—so that **one man was representing the entire Nation of Israel before God.**

This becomes a type of Jesus Christ, the believer's High Priest, who took on the form of flesh (which was also Resurrected) so that **one 'Man' now stands in the Presence of God to represent all of humanity!**

'Because God's children are human beings—made of flesh and blood—the Son also became flesh and blood. For only as a human could he die, and only by dying could he break the power of the devil, who had the power of death. Only in this way could he set free all who have lived their lives as slaves to the fear of dying.' (Hebrews 2:14 NLT)

Order of Jewels on the Breastplate of the High Priest (Exodus 39:8-21 NLT)		
Carnelian [Red]	**Peridot** [Lt. Green]	**Emerald**
Turquoise	**Lapis Lazuli** [Blue]	**White Moonshine**
Jacinth [Orange]	**Agate**	**Purple Amethyst**
Beryl [Blue-Green]	**Onyx**	**Green Jasper**

It is interesting to note that the above gemstones, although some names may vary, are identical to the Gemstones used to build the twelve Foundations of the New Jerusalem. (Revelation 21:19/20 NLT):

Jasper (1)	Sapphire (2)	Agate (3)
Emerald (4)	Onyx (5)	Carnelian (6)
Chrysolite (7)	Beryl (8)	Topaz/Peridot (9)
Chrysoprase (10)	Jacinth (11)	Amethyst (12)

Note the huge contrast between these two listings of Gemstones—twelve small gemstones compared to twelve massive layers of foundation stones!

The 'father' of faith, Abraham, was happy to live in tents, while he awaited the coming City of God; and Moses' Tabernacle—often called the 'tent in the Wilderness'—owed its continued existence to the annual appearance of the High Priest before God in the Holiest of Holies, where he offered a sin offering on behalf of all the people. **The names of the Tribes were engraved on these gemstones.**

In the Old Testament there was a priesthood of just one man—who is a 'type' of the New Jerusalem, whose twelve foundations are constructed from all those 'living stones' who have become 'priests unto God' through our Lord Jesus Christ. **The names of the Twelve Apostles were engraved on these foundations.** (Revelation 21:14)

'And you are living stones that God is building into his spiritual temple. What's more, you are his holy priests. Through the mediation of Jesus Christ, you offer spiritual sacrifices that please God.' (1 Peter 2:5 NLT).

The Five Offerings of Israel
Refer Leviticus chapters 1-7 for complex details about the procedure for each of these Offerings

1) **The Burnt Offering (Voluntary/Sweet Offering):**
   Animal totally burnt on Altar (except skin – given to Priests)
   Type of Christ: Surrendering Himself to God, to do God's Will 'as Christ also …(gave)… Himself for us, an offering and a sacrifice to God for a sweet-smelling aroma.' (Eph. 5:2)

2) **The Meal Offering (Voluntary/Sweet Offering):**
   Fine flour, oil and Frankincense, seasoned with salt (but no Leaven or Honey) Fried in a pan.
   Type of Christ: His sinless/pure humanity, full of the sweetness and fragrance of His life.

3) **The Peace Offering (Voluntary/Sweet Offering):**
   Animals blood, fat & kidneys burnt – but breast given to Aaron & sons and right shoulder to other priests.
   Type of Christ's Salvation: i.e. Both God and Man shared in this Offering. Both have a part to play in the work of Salvation in humanity i.e. Christ's Cross and my relationship with God.

4) **The Sin Offering** (**A Non-sweet offering**):
Bullock's blood and fat burnt on Altar – remainder of Bullock burnt on the ground *outside the Camp.*
Type of Christ: 'For (God) made Him who knew no sin to be sin for us, that we might become the righteousness of God in Him.' (II Cor. 5:21) Therefore: '… let us go forth to Him, *outside the camp*, bearing His reproach.' (Heb.13:13 italics added)

5) **The Trespass (aka as a Guilt) Offering** (**A Non-sweet offering**):
Ram's blood and fat burnt on Altar – Restitution for false dealings had to be made to the offended party on the same day the Offering was made – plus 20% was added to the amount restored.
Type of Christ: This offering is a 'type' of Christ who was crucified on behalf of our sins and trespasses. He has not only appeased the wrath of God by paying our sin-debt, but He has '*added 20%*' in that His Victory brought more glory to God and more blessings to man than either of them had before sin was introduced into heaven and earth.

The following Chart shows how the Five Offerings of Israel are themselves a 'type' of actions by Christ, the Messiah. In this Chart we also show that *in the reverse order these Offerings demonstrate the order by which a Believer comes to a maturity of faith in Christ.*

CHRIST ▼				BELIEVER ▲	
OFFERING:		◄TEXT	TEXT►		OFFERING:
BURNT	He fully submits to the Will of God	Phil. 2:6-8	Rom. 1:12	He fully submits to the Will of God	BURNT
MEAL	He lives a clean life	Heb. 9:14	I John 1:7	He lives a clean life	MEAL
PEACE	He makes Peace between God and Man by ...	Eph. 2:13-14	1 John. 1: 8/9	He finds Peace with God through Christ	PEACE
SIN	... taking Sin upon Himself ...	Isaiah 53:10-11	II Cor. 5:21	He learns about the provision of forgiveness by God	SIN
TRESPASS	... and dying for Man's sin-debt	Hebrews 9:26/28	I John. 2:1/2	He becomes aware of his need of a Saviour	TRESPASS

Chapter 8:

Menorah & the Seven Feasts of Israel
A Physical Description of the Menorah

Refer Exodus 25:31-40, 27:20/21 and 37:17-24

The Menorah was a large seven-stemmed oil-fueled Lamp in the Holy Place of the Tabernacle. It actually consisted of seven lamps—a larger lamp on top of the central stem of the Menorah, and six others atop its six branches. Historical accounts of its exact design vary greatly – but it is thought the central lamp resembled a basin, while the other six were shaped like boats, with their pointed ends facing into the Holy Place. Wicks were said to be created from worn-out priestly garments. The Menorah was to burn continuously and the wicks were trimmed morning and evening. (Exod.27:20/21)

Menorah of modern appearance

It was decorated with nine ornamental flowers, eleven ornamental fruit—and twenty-two smaller containers of oil. The Menorah was set on a solid base. All of this magnificent structure was created from only one piece of hammered gold.

Gold is the most malleable of all metals. Just one gram of gold can be beaten into a paper-thin sheet measuring one square metre, which can then be pressed into any desired shape.

We are reminded that the suffering of the Lord Jesus, at the time of His crucifixion, allow Him to be described as 'beaten work'—especially in the light of Isaiah 53:3. His sufferings can be seen in the seven occasions when He lost blood in the hours surrounding His crucifixion:

Sweat great drops of blood	- Luke 22:45
Beard plucked out	- Isaiah 50:6
Back lashed with whip	- Mark 15:13 – Isaiah 50:6
Crown of Thorns in scalp	- Matt. 27:29 John 19:2
Nails in feet	- John 19:18
Nails in hands	- John 20:24-29
Side pierced with spear	- John 19:34

'... many were amazed when they saw him. His face was so disfigured he seemed hardly human, and from his appearance, one would scarcely know he was a man.' (Isaiah 52:14 NLT)

'... he was pierced for our rebellion, crushed for our sins. He was beaten so we could be whole. He was whipped so we could be healed.' (Isaiah 53:5 NLT)

The Meaning behind the Menorah

There is an expression often used to explain Typology: 'The New is in the Old concealed; the Old is in the New revealed.' This is particularly true of the Golden Menorah, which is an outstanding type of so many cherished New Testament truths …

The Menorah gives Light: The original Menorah was believed to have been about the height of an average man. Its seven bowls of oil would have provided the only light available in the windowless Holy Place. The Menorah therefore becomes a type of the real light of God in the world, and also within the inner part of our being.

As one of the major symbols of the nation of Israel it is also a reminder that they are called to be 'a light to the Gentiles.' (Isaiah 42:6 & 49:6).

In the New Testament Jesus uses the symbol of light to explain how His followers are to be 'the light of the world' (Matt.5:14) and again in John 8:12 Jesus declares that He is 'the light of the world. He who follows Me shall not walk in darkness, but have the light of life.' Jesus made this statement in the Temple, and many believe He would have been standing close to a huge temple menorah—adding significance to His words.

The Menorah has Seven branches: Seven is the number of completeness, and these branches are also an example of 'unity in diversity' in the same way that a rainbow has seven colours and a week has seven days. The churches of Revelation 2/3 are seven distinctly different 'congregations' but are essentially part of the one Body of Christ, His Bride.

The Menorah resembles a tree and in Jewish tradition it is a reminder of the Tree of Life, from which Adam and Eve were banned—but which is subsequently made available for access in Revelation 22. In this way the Menorah speaks of eternal life made available only through the blood of the Messiah.

The Menorah is decorated with Almond Blossom: The Menorah was a masterpiece, created (not assembled) from one huge piece of pure gold.

Its shape followed the design of the Almond Tree—and joins the Olive tree, Fig tree and Vine—becoming one of the four trees which signify the life and history of Israel.

But why decorate it with almond blossoms?

a) When Aaron's authority was questioned (Refer Number 17:1-11) his was the only one of 12 rods, placed in the tabernacle, which 'had sprouted and put forth buds, had produced blossoms and yielded ripe almonds' in just one night. This was God at His 'Resurrection' best!

b) The ministry of Jeremiah commences with a vision of an almond branch (Jeremiah 1:11/12) and there follows God's comment; 'I am ready to perform My word.' This is a play on the Hebrew word for 'almond' which can also mean: 'diligence'. Almond blossom is a reminder of God's determined faithfulness.

Zechariah's Vision of the Menorah: The prophet Zechariah was puzzled when shown a vision of a Menorah (chapter 4:1-7) being fed with oil from 'two Olive trees', one of each side of the Menorah.

'… the Old is in the New revealed!' … In Romans 11 the Apostle Paul describes Jews and Gentiles as two Olive trees, with the branches of the wild Gentile Olive being grated into the cultivated Jewish Olive tree. He further reminds us that through the Gospel both the original and the grated olive will draw their life from the one root system,

Paul teaches more about this new union of Jew and Gentile in Ephesians when he uses similar illustrations of 'growing into a holy temple' and 'one new man':

'But now in Christ Jesus you who once were far off have been brought near by the blood of Christ. For He Himself is our peace, who has made both one, and has broken down the middle wall of separation, having abolished in His flesh the enmity, that is, the law of commandments contained in ordinances, *so as to create in Himself one new man from the two*, thus making peace, and that He might reconcile them both to God in one body through the cross, thereby putting to death the enmity. And He came and preached peace to you who were afar off and to those who were near. For through Him *we both have access by one Spirit to the Father.*' (Ephesians 2:13-22 Italics added)

The Seven Feasts of Israel
[Refer: Exodus 23:14-17 – Leviticus 23 – Numbers 28/29]

The number seven is one of the most well-used and significant numbers mentioned in the Bible. We see this in the seven individual lampstands seen by Apostle John in Revelation 1:12/13 (with Jesus standing in their midst) – and the new Lampstand seen in Zechariah's vision (Zechariah 4:1-3). These visions are based upon the seven lamps of the Golden Menorah in the Tabernacle – and the Jewish people have always related the seven branches of this Menorah to the seven Feasts of Israel. Both the Menorah and the Feasts all point us to Jesus.

1] Feast of Passover:
Date: 10th-14th of Abib (or Nisan). This was the beginning of the Religious Year for the Jews.
The first lamp (from the left) represents Passover, when God delivered the Israelites from Egyptian slavery. Jesus was the Passover lamb who rode into Jerusalem on 10th of Abib, the day the Passover lamb was inspected for any impurity, before being sacrificed on the 14th day of Abib. ***Jesus died on the Passover date, as God's Passover Lamb!***

2] Feast of Unleavened Bread:
Date: 15th day of Abib/Nisan.
The second lamp is Unleavened Bread (a feast day when you ate bread without yeast – and continued to do so for the next seven days). On this day the Jews prayed that God would 'bring fruit out of the ground that you most needed' for the following day of First fruits. ***Christ was in the tomb on this day*** and Messiah's resurrection would bring the answer to this prayer!

3] Feast of First Fruits:
Date: 16th day of Abib/Nisan.
The third lamp is First Fruits, which occurred three days after Passover. On this day (three days after Passover) the Jewish people brought God the first thing out of the ground from the spring harvest. ***Messiah was resurrected on this day!*** 'But now is Christ risen and become the first fruits of those who have fallen asleep.' (I Cor. 15:20/23)

> **Note: These three Feasts occurred in the months of March and April over a period of eight days, to celebrate the Barley harvest – known collectively as Passover.**

4] Feast of Pentecost:
Date: 6ᵗʰ day of 3ʳᵈ Month (Sivan).
This is the fourth and central lamp on the Menorah. This bowl was larger than the others, and was used to feed the other lamps their oil supply. It is claimed this light never ran out of oil! This feast is celebrated fifty days after First Fruits, and is the same day God spoke from the mountain and gave the Ten Commandments to the Israelites. ***This is the day the Holy Ghost came to abide*** with and empower the Church.

> **Note: This feast was originally known as 'Harvest' but over time became known as 'Pentecost'. It was a one-day Festival which occurred during the months of May/June, and signaled the commencement of the wheat harvest.**

5] Feast of Trumpets:
Date: 1st day of 7th month (Tishri). This was the first month of the Jewish Civil Year. Known as ***Rosh Hashanah***, Represented by the fifth lamp, this was a day for blowing trumpets (the ***Shofar***). This instrument was blown to announce Victory or the returning of a victorious king. Jesus said that He will one day return to earth as a king with the sound of trumpets.

Tradition says that some well-known people were born on this day: **Abraham** (1ˢᵗ Patriarch), **Isaac** (first persona associated with sacrificial lamb), **Jacob** (1ˢᵗ Tribe) and **Samuel** (1ˢᵗ Prophet). It is also considered to be the day when King Solomon dedicated the Temple.

6] The Day of Atonement:
Date: 10th day of the 7th Month (Tishri).
The sixth lamp represents the most sacred day of the year –known as *Yom Kippur* – when the High Priest placed his hands on the 'scapegoat', which was then released into the wilderness to represent the transfer of the people's sins on to the animal. After this the High Priest would go into the Holy of Holies and sprinkle the blood of another slain goat on the Mercy Seat, to 'cover' the sins of the people for another year.

7] Feast of Tabernacles:
Date: Celebrated for seven days **from 15ᵗʰ day of the 7ᵗʰ month (Tishri).** Known as *Sukkot*, this is the last day of the Religious Year.
This seventh light of the Menorah is considered to be the most important light, and points to the Feast of Tabernacles. In contrast to the earlier day of Atonement or Mourning, it was a time of great rejoicing and celebration at the end of the main harvests of the agricultural year, during which families lived in booths, or tent-like structures made from tree branches.

This feast occurred in the Northern Hemisphere Autumn period, a time when shepherds were 'living out in the fields …' (Luke 2:8), which tells us Jesus was born during this period.

Tabernacles was a celebration of God's light coming into the world. Family groups celebrated with giant candles symbolic of a modern-day birthday cake, and at one time King Herod created a giant-sized Menorah to stand in the temple area during Tabernacles. It is thought that at the lighting of this huge Menorah, Jesus may have proclaimed the famous words 'I am the light of the world.' (John 8:12)

More than anything else it was a time of rejoicing in the provision of God—as when an Angel of the Lord told the shepherds, 'Do not be afraid ... I bring you *good tidings of great
joy* which will be to all people. For there is born to you this day
... a Saviour who is Christ the Lord.' (Luke 2:10/11)

> **Note: These last three feasts occurred during September and
> October over a period of 21 days – celebrating the harvest
> of fruit like Grapes, Olives, Dates and Figs. They are known
> collectively as Tabernacles.**

Chapter 9:

Old Testament Individuals who were Types of Christ

Abel: A type of Christ – being the first person to suffer for righteousness sake (Matt. 23:34-35). Similarity and contrast with his and Christ's blood (Heb. 11:4; 12:24).

Abraham: A type of Christ in that he was the original stranger and foreigner (Gen.23:4), with 'nowhere to lay his head' (Luke 9:58) – becoming the father of many nations.

Adam: A type of Christ in that he represented humanity. Similarity and contrast with his and Christ's body (I Cor.15).

David: A type of Christ in that he was the shepherd from Bethlehem who became the King of Israel. The Redeemer is called 'David' (Ezekiel 34:23-24; 37:24-25).

Elijah: While Elijah is seen as a type of John Baptist—Jesus also called the covenant people to repentance; and was both hated and feared by the King (Herod).

Elisha: A type of Christ in that he was greater than the one (John Baptist) who preceded him.

Enoch: A type of Christ in that 'he walked with God and was not' and prefigured the bodily resurrection and ascension of Christ.

Ezra and Nehemiah: Both are types of Christ. Ezra, in that he re-built the spiritual life of Jerusalem, and Nehemiah, in that he rebuilt the walls of protection around the City. Jesus is the 'greater Nehemiah' who would not cease building the walls until they were finished (Neh.6:2-3). Jesus cried: 'It is finished' (John 19:30).

Isaac: A type of Christ in that he was born 'supernaturally' – and figuratively raised from the dead (Hebrews 11:19).

Jacob: A type of Christ in that he was named 'Israel' – so that Israel was a Person before giving birth to a Nation of that name.

Jeremiah: A type of Christ in that he also experienced a figurative death and resurrection when thrown into a pit and brought out (Lam. 3:52-57). He was a Prophet of sorrow and acquainted with grief.

Job: Job experienced a righteous suffering that has its antitype in Christ's suffering.

Jonah: A type of Christ in that he (like Isaac) experienced a '*typical*' death and resurrection.

Joseph: A type of Christ in that he suffered unjustly and was then exalted to rescue his brothers.

Judges: All Judges are types of Christ; in that they were deliverers and redeemers of God's oppressed people.

Melchizedek: was a type of Christ in that he was the King/ Priest who blessed Abraham.

Moses: Like Christ, Moses had a supernatural deliverance at birth; went down into Egypt – came out of Egypt – went through the water - into the wilderness and up on the mountain to give God's people the law. Jesus, likewise, leads His people out of the bondage of sin and death through His own 'exodus' (Luke 9:31 NLT).

Noah: Noah's name means 'rest' and he is a type of Christ in that he left the Ark to bring rest from the curse on the ground, and provide a 'new creation' for his family – as did Christ!

Samson: Although he is a much-maligned Bible character he was, in fact, a type of Christ in that he defeated more of God's enemies in his death than in his life!
[*For a further understanding of Samson refer Chapter Ten*]

Seth: His brother Abel is a type of grief but Seth, in contrast, is a type of Christ's resurrection, in that he replaced his brother (Gen. 4:25).

Solomon: A type of Christ in that he was the 'son of David.' Christ is the absolute son of David as well as being 'Christ the power of God and the wisdom of God.' (I Corinthians 1:24)

Chapter 10:

Types Located in Old Testament Books

In this chapter we will take a ***Types and Shadows Walk*** through the Old Testament, stopping to examine some of the major examples of types to be discovered. As this book is intended to be an appetiser only, rather than a three-course banquet, not all books will be examined.

When the discouraged disciples walking the road to Emmaus, had their encounter with Jesus (Luke 24:13--27), Cleopas and his companion (*whom Church tradition suggests was Luke the Beloved Physician*) reported that 'beginning at Moses and all the prophets, (Jesus) expounded to them in all the Scriptures the things concerning Himself.' (vs.27) There is every reason to think this would have included teaching that is often called 'types and shadows' in our modern world!

In the Jewish Bible the Old Testament (known as the *Tanakh*) is in a different order to the classic King James Bible. It is divided into three specific sections i.e. 'Moses' or the *Torah*, which is the first five books—Genesis to Deuteronomy—followed by the writings of the *Prophets;* and concluding with the *Other Writings*.

Jewish Rabbis have always accepted the significance of their scriptures; some believing that even the placement of individual letters has its own significance. Notice the criticism of Jesus by the Jews while He was teaching in the Temple during the Feast of Tabernacles: 'the Jews marvelled, saying, "How does this Man know letters, having never studied?"' (John 7:15)

Not all Old Testament books are examined in this chapter, but students are encouraged to read the unexamined books, locating and confirming other types for themselves.

Part One: Genesis to Esther

GENESIS –

The Life and Times of Isaac is a Type of:

a) The **Church** as it is comprised of Spiritual Children of Abraham (Refer Genesis chapters 17 and 21)

b) **Christ** – who was a Son obedient unto death (Refer Genesis 22:4-9)

c) **Christ** – as a Bridegroom (Refer Genesis 22:20 & chapter 24)

d) The New Nature of the Believer – '*born according to the Spirit*' (Galatians 4:29)

Comparisons between Joseph and Esther:

THE AMAZING COMPARISONS BETWEEN THE STORY OF JOSEPH AND ESTHER
Joseph and Esther rise to prominence in much the same way — both of them struggled against adversity to become a 'Saviour' of their people.

JOSEPH (Genesis 37-48)	ESTHER (Esther 1-10)
Lived in a foreign land (Egypt) - like an undercover agent for God!	**Lived in a foreign land** (Persia) - like an undercover agent for God!
Joseph hated by his brothers … and is sold to the Midianites for **20 pieces of silver** (37:28)	**Esther hated by Haman** who offers all the Jews of Persia for **20,000 pieces of silver**. (3:9). 'We have been sold, my people and I, to be destroyed …' (7:4)
Joseph gained a position with Potiphar, the captain of Pharaoh's guard – and Joseph **'found favour in his sight.'** (39:4)	Esther takes a step toward becoming Queen in Persia when she pleased the king's eunuch, Hegai, and **'she obtained his favour.'** (2:9). ▼
However, after an initial similarity, Esther's story confronts an unwanted adversary in the person of Haman the Agagite …	

Pharaoh gives authority to Joseph: 'Pharaoh took his signet ring off his hand and put it on Joseph's hand …' (41:42).	'So the king **took his signet ring** from his hand and **gave it to Haman** … (with authority) to annihilate all the Jews …' (3:10 & 13)
	… But GOD!
▼	Esther invites the King and Haman to a feast, where she exposes Haman's plot to kill all Jews (including Esther) … resulting in Haman being hanged on his own gallows. (7:1-10)
Because of this favour Joseph is able to instruct Pharaoh to 'let Pharaoh … **appoint officers over the land to collect (grain**) … in the seven plentiful years …' (41:34-35).	Esther had gained great favour with the King since the king's attendants advise him to '**appoint officers in all the provinces … (and) gather all the beautiful young virgins** … into the women's quarters' (2:3)

The 'officers' in **Persia 'gather'** *women* in the same way 'officers' in **Egypt 'collect'** *grain!* … highlighting their low regard for females, which Esther must overcome to fulfil her destiny and save her people.
So, the grain gathered in Egypt and the young virgins gathered in Persia become the means by which Joseph and Esther rescue their own people.

EXODUS –

The Paschal Lamb (Refer Notes in Chapter One)

LEVITICUS –

The Five Offerings of Israel – for full details refer to 'The Five Offerings of Israel' in Chapter 7.

NUMBERS –

Manna (Chapter 11) A Type of God's provision of 'spiritual meat'. See also: I Corinthians 10:3 and John 6:31-36 'spiritual meat' and 'bread from heaven.'

Smitten Rock (Chapter 20) A Type of God's provision of 'spiritual drink' and 'spiritual food'. Refer I Corinthians 10:3.

Note: This particular Type can also be used to speak of water as a type of the Holy Spirit: 'the gift of God' or 'living water'.

See John 4 and John 7:37. Christ is not offering Himself, but the Spirit of God, who is typified by the illustration of water.

Brazen Serpent (Chapter 21) See also John 3:14/15

Question: Why would you use a serpent—a symbol of evil—to represent a healing source for the people?

Answer: This is an amazing type of Christ, the Saviour from sin. Christ became sin for us i.e. being punished as a criminal He looked like the sin He came to conquer! The serpent was also made of brass, the same substance as the Altar of Sacrifice in the Tabernacle.

DEUTERONOMY –

The Six Cities of Refuge

(Refer Deuteronomy 19 and Joshua 20)

Ancient Israel's six Cities of Refuge are a type of the 'refuge' the Christian believer can find in Jesus Christ.

They were 'appointed for all the children of Israel and for the stranger … that whoever killed a person accidentally may flee there, and not die by the hand of the avenger of blood until he stood before the congregation.' (Joshua 20:9)

The cities of **Kedesh, Shechem** and **Hebron** were located of the western side of the Jordan river (from north to south) and the cities of **Golan, Ramoth-gilead** and **Bezer** were likewise located on the eastern side of Jordan (from north to south).

A man fleeing to a City of Refuge, once accepted by the City Fathers, must wait until the death of the High Priest for his actual release (Joshua 20:6) – **however, our High Priest has already died!**

JOSHUA (The Book) –

Note: The River Jordan must not be taught as a type of physical death; any more than Canaan is a legitimate type of a future Heaven—because there are no giants or enemies to be conquered in Heaven!

Jordan and Canaan are best seen as a type of the Believer being Water Baptised into the death/life of Christ, so they are enabled to fight against the enemies of the Christian life experience.

JOSHUA (The Man) –

Joshua, the man, is a type of Christ as the 'Captain of our Salvation.' His name means 'Jehovah-Saviour'.

i)   Joshua comes *after* Moses, in the sense that the **Law** came by Moses (John 1:17) . . . but **Grace** came by Jesus Christ . . . '

ii)   Joshua leads to Victory, in the sense that the Law failed – now Joshua is required to lead us into the Promised Land.

iii)   Joshua is our Advocate when we have suffered defeat. (After the defeat of Ai Joshua interceded for God's people). Refer I John 2:1 'we have an advocate with the Father, Jesus Christ the righteous.'

iv)   Joshua allots portions to the people – 'in whom we have obtained an inheritance.' Ephesians 1:11. (Ephesians 4:8-11 speaks of the Ministry Gifts of Christ which He gives.)

Crossing Jordan (Chapters 3 & 4)

a)   A type of Christ's Intercession is seen in the Priests who stood in Jordan until everyone had passed over.

b)   Also seen as a type of our death in Christ. (I Corinthians 10:1-4)

c)   Stones **brought into the riverbed** (Joshua 4:9) represent the old life, which is buried in Water Baptism – left in the River, and covered by the tide forever!

d)   Stones **taken from the Riverbed** represent our new life in Christ. Notice these are stones of the same basic substance as the stones taken into the river, but they are different. They are stones which have been 'resurrected from death.' (Note: these stones may have had a smoother appearance than land-based stones used to build other memorials.)

Inheritance (Chapters 13-21)

The land was allotted to them by Joshua, but it was necessary for them to fight for the full possession of their inheritance!

The 'Rest' of the Promised Land

'Then the land rested from war' (Joshua 11:23). The New Testament reports that Joshua did not give them true, lasting rest: therefore, this Joshua 11:23 'rest' becomes a type of the **true rest** which we have in Jesus Christ.

READ Hebrews 4:1-11. We have ceased from our own 'works' and are rested in Christ.

JUDGES –

The purpose of the Judges was to deliver Israel from their enemies and to restore their social and spiritual life, after the nation's loss of faith had opened a way for them to be defeated. This occurred on numerous occasions—the most prominent being their subjection to the Philistines. A study of the life of a notable Judge—Samson—opens up some surprising comparisons with the life of Jesus Christ.

Samson as a Type of Christ

The life of Samson has been depicted in everything from movies to cartoons, while being described by some—because of his moral failures—as 'the weakest strong man who ever lived'.

However, we must never forget that after being called by God from before his birth, he fulfilled his purpose by ruling as an esteemed Judge over Israel for a period of twenty years (mentioned twice in Judges 15:20 & 16:31). Early in his life his Jewish parents could not understand his desire to marry a non-Jewish woman, although in doing so *'he was seeking an occasion to move against the Philistines*.' (Judges 14:4). Indeed, this was to fulfil the words of the Angel when prophesying his birth to his mother, that Samson would *'begin to deliver Israel out of the hands of the Philistines*.' (Judges 13:5).

Perhaps the greatest accolade given to Samson is that he is included by name in Hebrews 11:32 as a **man of great faith**.

In that chapter other phrases like: '*who through faith subdued kingdoms*' and '*stopped the mouths of lions*' and '*out of weakness were made strong*' all rightfully apply to Samson.

Samson at his death was Samson at his finest; and in this way he becomes an amazing type of Christ. The following Chart seeks to illustrate many other ways in which Samson's life demonstrates prophetic parallels with the life of Jesus Christ.

SAMSON (Judges 13-16)	CHRIST
Birth announced by Angel to his mother (13:3-5)	Birth announced by Angel to His mother (Luke 1:26-38)
Birth unexpected - mother was barren (13:2-3)	Birth was unexpected – mother was a virgin (Luke 1:34)
Israel under the power of Philistines (10:7/8; 13:1)	Israel under the power of Rome (Luke 1:5)
Samson married a Gentile - Christ died for the 'Bride of Christ' – thus joining Jew and Gentile into 'one new man'. (Eph. 2:14-18 & Col. 3:10-11)	
With great strength & courage Samson kills a lion (Judges 14:5-6)	Christ destroyed our adversary the devil – 'who is *like a roaring lion*' (I Peter 5:8)
In removing the Gates of the city in Gaza (Judg.16:1-3) it must be assumed that he first killed the men at the gates. This action is a type of Christ possessing the gates of His enemies through the Cross. Samson also carried the gates some (20 miles/32 kms) to Hebron – the place where 'Father Abraham' (the father of faith) was buried.	
Samson sincerely loved a woman (Delilah) who betrayed him for money. (16:18)	Jesus showed love to the man (Judas) who betrayed Him for money. (Mark 14:42)

Samson lays down his authority by having his seven locks of hair shaved (16:17/19)	Jesus lays down His authority - founded in the Seven Spirit of God. (Isaiah 11:2)
Samson's is given women's work in prison - grinding at the mill. (16:21)	The Lord Jesus was greatly humiliated. (Acts 8:32/33).
Samson not killed immediately, but tortured – perhaps to be later offered as a sacrifice to Dagon. (16:23)	Jewish leadership tried to kill Jesus many times – before torturing him prior to his crucifixion.
Samson died between two stone pillars. (16:25-26)	Jesus died between two crosses. (John 19:18)
Samson pulls down the building, 'So the dead which he slew at his death were more than they which he slew in his life.' (16:30)	Through his own death, Christ destroyed the power of sin, bringing Salvation to the world.
After his death 'His brothers & all his father's household came down and took him up and buried him.' (16:31)	Jesus was buried by Joseph and Nicodemus. (John 19:38-42)

The above Chart makes no mention of the three major physical victories Samson had over the Philistines—all of which can be considered as a type of the Victory gained by our Saviour, Jesus. Nor does the Chart include the incident with the jawbone of an Ass. After the battle, Samson is intensely thirsty and to quench his thirst, God splits open the ground where the jawbone is discarded, so that a supply of thirst-quenching water is revealed.

The comparison between Samson's thirst and Christ's thirst on the Cross is easy to observe—but Bible teacher [ii]Adrian Beale suggests there is also a comparison here to the outpouring of the Holy Spirit on the Day of Pentecost, and the subsequent experience of speaking with Other Tongues i.e. refreshing water flows from the speaking-bone ('jawbone') of an animal.

I & 2 SAMUEL, I & 2 KINGS and I & 2 CHRONICLES

The books of 1st and 2nd Samuel, together with 1st and 2nd Kings are among the 'Prophetic' books in the Jewish Bible—while 1st and 2nd Chronicles are located among the 'Other Writings'. They were originally three large scrolls, which were each divided into two smaller scrolls at a later date and, because of this, Samuel's name is only found in 1st Samuel.

Although Chronicles appears to be a repeat of Kings, it deals only with the history of the Kings of Judah, only mentioning Israel in passing.

These books tell the story of numerous characters, most of whom played a rulership/kingly role in the early history of God's people—affecting their political, military, economic and religious life. We learn of Samuel, who was himself the last of the Judges as well as being a Prophet. Mention is also made of people like Saul, David, Solomon, Mephibosheth, Elijah and Elisha, Jehu and numerous kings of both good and evil reputation.

They all have various types associated with their story, many of whom are mentioned elsewhere in this book. We have left plenty of ground for eager students to pursue their own research.

Special Note: The Books of **EZRA, NEHEMIAH and ESTHER** are all concerned with the Return of the Jews to their own land, after the Babylonian Captivity. The order in which these books appear in the Scriptures reflects God's perspective, rather than the time-line of actual history i.e. (**1**) Ezra records the re-building of the Temple; (**2**) Nehemiah tells the story of the re-building of the walls and the establishment of life in Jerusalem; while (**3**) Esther tells of the preservation of the people from Hamon's plans for Jewish genocide! Note: from the perspective of the timing of history their order would be: **Esther, Nehemiah and Ezra.**

ESTHER –

Esther can be seen as a type of Christ:

ESTHER:	CHRIST:
Esther begins her Fast on the 14th Nisan – which is also the beginning of Passover	Christ died on 14th Nisan
Fasting in O.T. is considered to be an affliction and a sacrifice. (Lev. 23:27, 29; cf. Ps. 35:13; 69:10)	Christ was afflicted for us (Phil.2:1-8)
Esther ends her Fast on 3rd day = 16th of Nisan.	Christ was Resurrected on 3rd day = 16th of Nisan
Esther 'put on royalty' to approach the king	Christ was glorified to ascend the Throne of Heaven

This is the story of how a young Jewish girl marries a Gentile King and delivers the Kingdom from a great disaster.

The story of Esther can also be understood as a 'type' of a man/woman living in such a way as to give the Holy Spirit such influence in their life that the so-called 'works of the flesh' (as per Romans 5-8) are defeated and eliminated:

- **King Ahasuerus** – is a 'type' of a Man, his soul and his decision-making capacity. The whole story revolves around the decisions of the King, and their widespread effect on the Palace, the City of Shushan and the 127 Provinces of the Persian Empire.

- **Queen Vashi** – is a 'type' of a Man's human/natural spirit which, like Vashti, can be rebellious and disobedient. On the other hand, it is obvious that the King fails to give proper attention to his spirit, as depicted in his divorce from Vashti.

- **Queen Esther** – As Esther replaces Vashti, she is a 'type' of a person's new, regenerated spirit, after converting to Christ. Initially the King does not realise the strong influence that Esther is having on him, until he later invites her to exert influence upon his life.

- **Esther's Uncle Mordecai** – Most of Esther's decisions are influenced by her cousin Mordecai, who is a 'type' of the Holy Spirit. His 'knowledge' saves the King from an assassination plot, and Mordecai also works behind the scenes to ensure the defeat of the villain Haman.

- **Haman the villain** – is the enemy of all that is good in the Kingdom of Ahasuerus, and is a type of the old sinful nature and the 'works of the flesh', which are constantly at war with the activity of Mordecai (the Holy Spirit). Victory is gained when Haman is unmasked and he and his ten sons are hanged on gallows in the public square.

Part Two: Job to Malachi

The following books of JOB, PSALMS, PROVERBS, ECCLESIASTES and the SONG OF SOLOMON are considered to be the Poetic books of the Old Testament. These five books contain a multitude of differing poetic styles – a few of which are discussed in some detail in Chapter Twelve.

JOB –

Some Bible students may not see types of Christ in the book of Job.

However, Jesus Himself said: 'These are the words which I spoke to you while I was with you, that all things must be fulfilled which were written in the Law of Moses and the Prophets and the Psalms concerning Me. And He opened their understanding, that they might comprehend the Scriptures.' (Luke 24:44-45)

In the Jewish mind the phrase 'the Psalms' includes all of the above five poetic books of the Bible.

Understood correctly, the entire Old Testament is written to introduce us to Jesus Christ; which is why the concept of Typology becomes such an important tool to identify and release this revelation to our hearts.

Bible Teacher [iii]Bob Sorge suggests the following similarities between the experiences of Job and Jesus:

Job's early success has an amazing similarity to Christ's early ministry; his trial to Christ's death; and his restoration to Christ's Resurrection!	

JOB (Chapters 1-42)	JESUS CHRIST
A 'blameless and upright man' suffers much. (1:8)	Just like Christ
'Naked I came ... naked shall I return' (1.21)	Jesus died naked on a cross
Job's friends 'did not recognise him.' (2.12)	Jesus was 'marred more than any man.' (Isaiah 52:14)
His friend Eliphaz taunted Job (5:1) and levelled false charges against him (22:6-9)	Jesus was taunted (Matt.27:43) and faced false charges at His trial.
Job cried: 'O earth, do not cover my blood.' (16:18)	Christ's blood taken into heaven (Hebrews 9:11-22)
Job asked God: 'Why do you hide Your face ...' (13:24)	Jesus asked: 'My God, My God, why have You forsaken Me?' (Matt.27:46)
Job's friends could not understand why such suffering would fall on a man if he was as blameless as Job said he was!	The Jews could not believe that God could become a man and be cursed. 'Cursed is anyone who hangs on a tree.' (Gal.3:13)

PSALMS and PROVERBS –

These are poetic books, which employ numerous literary forms. (Refer Chapter Twelve for further details)

ECCLESIASTES –

There is no major 'type' in this book; but there is an interesting 'Allegory of the Old Man' in chapter 12:1-7.

'Keepers of the house tremble'	– joints lose strength
'Grinders cease'	– teeth decay
'The windows grow dim'	– poor eyesight
'Rising up at the sound of a bird'	– failure to sleep
'Daughters of music are brought low'	– loss of hearing
'Afraid of height'	– unsteady on feet
'Grasshopper is a burden'	– can't carry weights
'Desire fails'	– no longer desires rich food
'Pitcher shattered at the fountain'	– Death comes at last

(For further comments about Allegories, see Chapter Twelve)

SONG OF SOLOMON –

The entire book is a Prophetic Allegory of a Groom (Christ) searching for his Bride (The Church).

EZEKIEL –

Cherubim – Four-faced Heavenly Creatures (Chapter One)

It is important to note that only Cherubim and Seraphim have wings. **Angels do not have wings**. Seraphim and Cherubim are Heavenly Beings of great power and authority.

WINGS - expressing a higher sphere of sacrifice or worship.

EYES in front and behind – engaged in ceaseless vigilance, with a higher capacity for knowledge.

However, Cherubim possess a human form, but with four different faces, which have been interpreted in various ways:

MAN	- having the highest ideals of wisdom and knowledge
LION	- having majesty and power
OX	- creatures of great productivity and industry
EAGLE	- having dominion and irresistible might

As a 'Shadow' of the four Gospels:

LION   - Matthew – the Gospel of the Messiah
OX   - Mark – the Gospel of the Obedient Servant
MAN   - Luke – the Gospel of the Son of Man
EAGLE   - John – the Gospel of the Son of God

As a 'Shadow' of the Five-fold Ministry Gifts:

APOSTLE   - Matthew/Lion
PROPHET   - John/Eagle
EVANGELIST   - Mark/Ox
PASTOR/TEACHER   - Luke/Man

CHERUBIM	LOCATION
Guarding gateway to Eden	They stood **within** Paradise (Gen. 3:24) It was their Duty – to **preserve** the Garden
In the Tabernacle (a)	Two golden Cherubim **guarding** the Mercy Seat (Exodus 25:17-22)
In the Tabernacle (b) Woven into all Tabernacle curtaining	Cherubim are the **Guardians of the Throne of Heaven** (Revelation 4:6-11)
Ezekiel's Vision (Chap.1)	Cherubim lead us to the *****Glory of God in human form, seated on a Throne**
*(vs.26 'a likeness with the appearance of a man' . . . vs.28 'the appearance of the likeness of the glory of the Lord.')	
Cherubim in Heaven (Revelation chaps. 4 & 5)	Ezekiel's Cherubim are found **'in the midst … and around'** the Throne of God in Heaven. A further type of Redeemed Humanity giving praise to God.

DANIEL -

Among Christians, Daniel is referred to as 'the Prophet Daniel.' However, the Jewish Scriptures place him among the 'Other Writings' rather than among the Prophets. They accept that while Daniel interpreted dreams for the king, and he also described some amazing visions and dreams about future events, he was not a 'prophet' in the sense that he spoke messages which he had received directly from God.

However, Daniel is clearly a 'type' of Christ in some amazing ways:

DANIEL (Chapter Six)	CHRIST (Matthew 27/28)
Accused on a trumped-up charge	Accused on a trumped-up charge
The King seeks to deliver him	Pilate attempts to free Him
Daniel is condemned to death	Jesus is condemned to death
Placed in a Lion's Den with a stone laid on the opening	Placed in a tomb with a stone laid at the opening
At daybreak his friends found he had been delivered from death	At daybreak women/disciples discovered he had been resurrected from death

THE MINOR PROPHETS

There is not a lot of activity in the books known as the 'Minor Prophets'—mostly preaching—so that types are not so plentiful. **Special Note:** The term 'minor' refers only in the length of the prophet's recorded prophecies, but not in his personal impact on Israel.

There are twelve of these books, and the number twelve is associated with government and God's authority. For their size these books are well quoted in the New Testament and in the list that follows I have given the cross-references between these books and the New Testament quotes.

Notice also how the names of the prophet relate strongly to the content of their prophecies.

HOSEA – Name means 'salvation'. He wrote primarily to the Northern Kingdom and as his name suggests, he sought Israel's salvation through their repentance.

[Hosea 1:10 & 2:23 quoted in Romans 9:25/26 - Hosea 10:8 quoted in Luke 2:30 – Hosea 11:1 quoted in Matt.2:15 – Hosea 6:7 quoted in Matt.9:13, and Hosea 13:14 quoted in 1 Corinthians 15:55]

JOEL – Name means 'Jehovah is Lord'. He wrote about the coming Day of the Lord—and is quoted at length by Apostle Peter on the Day of Pentecost, as he validates the experience of the Holy Ghost Baptism.

[Joel 2:28-32 quoted in Acts 2:17-20]

AMOS – Name means 'to be born (or carried) by God'. He prophesied against the reliance on wealth, rather than God, in the Northern Kingdom. He is powerfully quoted by Apostle James in Acts chapter 15 in his support for the inclusion of Gentiles into the church of God—and by the Martyr Stephen in his defense against the charge of blasphemy.

[Amos 5:25-27 quoted in Acts 7:42/43 – Amos 9:11/12 quoted in Acts 15:16/17]

OBADIAH – Name means 'Servant of God'. He wrote to support Judah when they were being attacked by their enemies; assuring them that God still cared for them.

There are no New Testament quotes from Obadiah.

JONAH – Name means 'Peace' or 'Dove'. Jonah's resistance to the Call of God to preach to Gentile Nineveh ended when swallowed by a great sea creature. Although not quoted in the New Testament the story of God's mercy to repentant Nineveh adds to the Old Testament's prophetic insistence that Salvation will eventually be available to the whole world.

Although **there are no New Testament quotes from Jonah**, Jesus refers to him as a type of his own 'three days and three night in the heart of the earth.' (Matt.12:40)

MICAH – Name means 'Who is like God?' He preached against social injustice, greed and political corruption; warning against the coming Assyrian attacks.

[Micah 5:2 quoted in Matt.2:6 – Micah 7:6 quoted in Matt. 10:35/36]

NAHUM – Name means 'Comforter'. His preaching assures Israel that God is aware of their troubles and ultimately justice will prevail. Just trust Him.

[Nahum 1:15 alluded to in Romans 10:15, although the full text is from Isaiah 52:7]

HABAKKUK – Name means 'Embrace'. This prophet assures the people of the certainty of God's coming and that He will judge the nations who oppose His purpose. Habakkuk's statement 'The just shall live by faith' (2:4) is famously requoted three times in the New Testament.

[Habakkuk 1:5 quoted in Acts 13:41 – Habakkuk 2:3/4 quoted in Romans 1:17, Galatians 3:11 and Hebrews 10:37]

ZEPHANIAH – Name means 'Hidden by God'. Although this prophet speaks about great doom and destruction, he also pre-dicts: 'In that day it shall be said to Jerusalem...The Lord your God is in your midst, the Might One, will save; He will rejoice over you with gladness, He will quiet you with His love, He will rejoice over you with singing.' (Zephaniah 3:16-18)

Zephaniah is not quoted in the New Testament.

HAGGAI – Name means 'Festive'. This unusually named proph-et urges the people involved in the re-building of Jerusalem, to put the building of God's House above building their own houses, so that God's presence will bring blessings to them—and they will become 'festive'!

[Haggai 2:7 is quoted in Hebrews 12:26]

ZECHARIAH – Name means 'Remembered by God'. The name of this prophet is a reminder to God's people that He will not forget His own, as Zechariah's name means "remembered by God."

Zechariah's strong prophetic preaching predicts, among other things, the coming Messiah (2:5 & 10) and of Christ riding a donkey into Jerusalem (9:9-10). He is well quoted in the New Testament.

[Zechariah 3:2/3 is quoted in Jude 9 – Zechariah 8:16 is quoted in Ephesians 4:25 – Zechariah 9:9 is quoted in Matt.21:5 – Zechariah 11:12 is quoted in Matt. 27:9 – Zechariah 12:10 is quoted in John 19:37 – and Zechariah 13:7 is quoted in Matt. 26:31 and Mark 14:27]

MALACHI – Name means 'My (God's) Messenger.' In this book the Lord is concerned that His people are not paying their tithes, nor are they paying their workers the correct wage. (Malachi 3:1-8). Malachi prophesies that Elijah will come again just before the day of the Lord (4:5-6) —fulfilled in the coming of John the Baptist, who came in the spirit of Elijah. (Mark 1:4; Matt 3:1). [Malachi 1:2/3 is quoted in Romans 9:13 – Malachi 3:1 is quoted in Matt. 11:10, Mark 1:2 and Luke 7:27 – and Malachi 4:6 is quoted in Luke 1:17]

Chapter 11:

New Testament Typology

Parabolic Types from Matthew chapter 13

In telling these Parables, Jesus is sitting in a boat on the sea of Galilee—the sea becoming a type Gentile Nations (sea powers). However, His Parables about sowing seed in the field (the 'field' representing the world) is contrary to Jewish expectation of a Messiah, exclusively for the benefit of the Nation of Israel. If the Kingdom of Heaven only referred to Israel, one would expect to hear a Parable about an Olive tree for instance.

The Kingdom of Heaven must be understood as pure Christianity in the Earth. These Parables are divided into two groups:

(A) Those spoken to the Crowds

- **Sower**: Not all seed sown bears fruit! (World, Flesh and Devil). Not all men will be converted before the end of the age.

- **Wheat and Tares**: This seed is the good seed of the first Parable. Wheat and Tares look alike—so do believers and hypocrites! Tares are specifically seen as being the 'children of the devil', rather than being unbelievers generally. (Refer Matt.13:28, 23:15 and John 8:38-44).

- **Mustard Seed**: Rapid but abnormal development of Christendom to a great place in the earth. (Note: Mustard 'tree' is no more than a shrub, and grows at its highest between eight and ten feet (2.5 to 3 metres). It is obvious that the Mustard tree in the parable has grown out of all proportion

> **Jesus never spoke to the crowds without using a Parable**
> • Matt. 13:34 •

to its natural counterpart. Birds—understood to be wicked men—will despoil the church.

- **Leaven**: Gospel will be mingled with false doctrines, increasing to the end of the age (particularly wrong doctrine about the Trinity.)

(B) Those spoken to the Disciples in the House

- **Treasure in the Field**:

  (a) This is a picture of the Church 'hidden' in the world and not recognised for its true value i.e. salt, light, 'the riches of the glory of His inheritance in the saints.' (Ephesians 1:18)

  (b) Note: Many teachers have spoken of this as 'Israel' being hidden in the earth, but this does not fit the idea of these parabolic types referring to the Kingdom in the world.

- **The Pearl**:
  Note: *We* have not found the 'pearl of greatest price'—Christ, the Pearl, has found *us*!
  This Pearl is the Church: Pearls come from the sea i.e. from Gentile Nations. Grains of sand create a wound in the side of the Oyster. The Oyster deposits a thin crust of a bright substance around the grain of sand, repeating the process until the pearl is formed, blending the colours of the rainbow. Figuratively, the Church was taken out of the wounded side of Christ.

- **The Dragnet**:
  Similar to the Wheat and the Tares. This is **not** to be used as a picture of a 'Gospel Net'! This parable refers to the end times when the 'men' or the 'reapers' will sort the good from the bad.

Parables of the Old Testament

**For a full listing of Old Testament Parables refer:
Appendix B**

The 'I Am' Statements of Jesus

The confrontation between Jesus and the Jews in John chapter 8 came to a head in vss.56-59 when Jesus made the amazing claim: 'Your father Abraham rejoiced to see My day, and he saw it and was glad.' The Jews immediately challenged His claim to have seen Abraham and asked: 'Have You seen Abraham?'—to which Jesus replied: *'Most assuredly, I say unto you, before Abraham was I Am.'*

By this statement Jesus was making the claim that He was God, and **was therefore part of every 'I AM' statement God had ever made.** His statement resulted in the Jews picking up stones to throw at Him … 'but Jesus hid Himself and went out of the temple, going through the midst of them, and so passed by.' (John 8:59)

In the following Charts we take a look at the amazing 'I AM' statements in Genesis, the Psalms, John's Gospel, and in the book of Revelation—all involving multiples of 'Seven'.

GENESIS:	'I AM' STATEMENTS:
	Spoken to Abraham:
15:1/7	*'Do not be afraid, Abram. I am your shield, your exceedingly great reward ... I am the LORD, who brought you out of Ur . . . to give you this land to inherit it.'*
17:1	'I am Almighty God; walk before Me and be blameless.'
	Spoken to Isaac:
26:24	'I am the God of your father Abraham; do not fear, for I am with you.'
	Spoken to Jacob:
28:13	'I am the LORD God of Abraham your father and the God of Isaac.'
31:13	'I am the God of Bethel, where you anointed the pillars and where you made a vow to Me.'
35:11	'I am God Almighty. Be fruitful and multiply ...'
46:3	'I am God, the God of your father; do not fear to go down to Egypt, for I will make of you a great nation there.'

PSALMS:	'I AM' STATEMENTS:

The Psalms mentioned below are known as 'Messianic Psalms' because they are all quoted in the New Testament. They speak of the future sufferings of Messiah.

22:6	*'But I am a worm, and no man ...'*
40:17	*'But I am poor and needy; ,,,'*
69:8	*'I (am) have become a stranger to my brothers ...'*
69:20	*'I am full of heaviness; ...'*
69:29	*'I am poor and sorrowful; ...'*
102:7	*'I ... am like a sparrow alone on the house top.'*
102:11	*'I (am) wither away like grass.'*

JOHN:	'I AM' STATEMENTS:

The structure of John's Gospel is very unique – and part of this uniqueness is the recording of the seven 'I AM' statements located in the Gospel.

6:35, 48 & 51	*'I am the bread of life ... I am the bread of life ... I am the living bread which came down from heaven ...'*
8:12	*'I am the light of the world. He who follows Me shall not walk in darkness, but have the light of life.'*
10:7 & 9	*'I am the door of the sheep ... I am the door.'*
10:11/14	*'I am the good shepherd.'*
11:25-26	*'I am the resurrection, and the life. He who believes in Me, though he may die, he shall live...'*
14:6	*'I am the way, the truth, and the life. No one comes to the Father except through Me.'*
15:1/5	*'I am the true vine, and My Father is the vinedresser ... I am the Vine, you are the branches.'*

REVELATION:	'I AM' STATEMENTS:
The Seven 'I AM' titles given to Jesus in the book of Revelation all speak of His Eternal Existence.	

1:8	*'I am Alpha and the Omega, the Beginning and the End, says the Lord, 'who is and who was and who is to come, the Almighty.'*
1:11	*'I am Alpha and the Omega, the First and the Last.'*
1:17	*'Do not be afraid; I am the First and the Last.'*
1:18	*'I am He who lives, and was dead, and behold, I am alive forevermore.'*
21:6	*'It is done! I am the Alpha and the Omega, the Beginning and the End ...'*
22:13	*'I am the Alpha and the Omega, the Beginning and the End, the First and the Last.'*
22:16	*'I am the Root and the Offspring of David, and the Bright and Morning Star.'*

Students who wish to explore the 'I AM' statements still further would do well to take a look at the research of [iv]Henry M. Morris Ph.D. of the Creation Research Society.

[Among other things, Morris reports there are 21 'I Am's in the Exodus – there are 35 'I Am's in Isaiah chapters 40-66 (which is 7x5) – there are 70 'I Am's in Ezekiel (which is 7x10) – and there are 21 'I Am's in Jeremiah (which is 7x3). His research further reports that all the prophetic books of the Old Testament contain a total of 154 'I am's (which is 7x22).]

Frank Harvey

In the New Testament we locate people like Apostles John and Peter, John Baptist – and Jesus Christ Himself – all making statements which declare that the life and Ministry of Jesus is the fulfilment of meaning expressed by Old Testament persons.

JESUS IN THE NEW TESTAMENT - SEEN AS THE FULFILMENT OF OLD TESTAMENT PERSONS/OBJECTS:

OT REF:	NAME:	NT REF:	QUOTE:
II Sam. 7:12/13	King SOLOMON	Luke 1:32-35 and Luke 11:31	1:32. 'He will be great, and .... the Lord will give Him **the throne of His father David**.' 11:31. '... she came from the ends of the earth to hear the wisdom of Solomon; and indeed a **greater than Solomon is here.**'
Exod. 40:2-34	The TABERNACLE	John 1:14 and Hebrews 9:11	1:14 'And the Word became flesh and dwelt among us ...', 9:11 'Christ came ... with **the greater and more perfect tabernacle** not made with hands ...
Exod.12:1-11	LAMB of GOD (Passover Lamb)	John 1:29 and 1 Peter 1:19	1:29 'John saw Jesus ... Behold! The Lamb of God ...' 1:19 '... **the precious blood of Christ, as of a lamb without blemish** ...'

94

Gen. 28:12	**JACOB'S LADDER**	John 1:51	1:51 Jesus: 'hereafter you shall see heaven open, & the **angels of God ascending and descending** upon the Son of Man.'
I Kings 6:1-38	**The TEMPLE**	John 2:19-21	2:19-21 'Destroy this temple … but He was speaking of **the temple of His body.**'
Exod. 16:4	**MANNA**	John 6 32-35 and John 6:48-51	6:33 '… the bread (*Manna*) of God is He who comes down from heaven and gives life to the world.' 6:51 '**I am the living bread** which came down from heaven …'
Exod. 30:7-8; 27:20; Prov. 4:18	**MENORAH**	John 8:12 Matt. 5:14-16; 2 Cor. 4:6; Eph.1:18; 5:13; Phil. 2:15-16	8:12 'I am the light of the world. He who follows Me shall not walk in darkness, but have the light of life.'
Gen. 2:9	**TREE OF LIFE**	John 14:6 & 15:1 and Rev. 22:2	14:6 'I am the way, the truth and the life …' 15:1 'I am the true vine …' 22:2 '… proceeding from the throne of … the Lamb … was **the tree of life …**'
Exod.17:6	**The ROCK**	John 7:37 I Cor.10:4	7:37 'If anyone thirsts, let him come to Me and drink …. out of his heart will flow rivers of living water.' 10:4 '… they drank of that spiritual Rock that followed them, and **that Rock was Christ.**'

Chapter 12:

Christ – Our Great High Priest

Christ is a Priest! This is one of the least understood facts of the Christian faith—and the greatest theme in the book of Hebrews.

> 'There is much more we would like to say about (Melchizedek), but it is difficult to explain, especially since you are spiritually dull and don't seem to listen. You have been believers so long now that you ought to be teaching others. Instead you need someone to teach you again the basic things about God's word.'
> (Hebrews 5:11 NLT)

There are priests in every realm; national, cultural and religious. These priests, witchdoctors, wizards etc. are always associated in some form with . . .

* a world-wide consciousness of sin of some form
* a supposed means of atonement or peace-making, with either a supreme being, or lesser gods or even with evil spirits.
* the avoidance of punishment and vengeful actions by evil powers and spirits

Protestants sometimes shy-away from the subject of 'priest-hood' because of what is seen in the heathen world and in the extremes of the Roman/

The least understood fact of the Christian faith!

Babylonian church, and their system of priesthood. However, the most perfect expression of Priesthood is found in Jesus Christ.

Proof of Christ's Priesthood (Hebrews 5 NLT)

The biblical facts of the priesthood of Christ are presented in Hebrews in contrast to the Jewish ceremonials, which are but a type of Christ anyway!

Christ is a priest

   a) in that he possessed our human nature with a capacity for empathy (5:1-3)

   i) The Aaronic priest was taken *from among* men, and ordained *for* men, in things pertaining to God. He must face two directions—man and God

   ii) The Aaronic priest must bear patiently with the ignorant and the erring. He must share a 'kinship' with them. He must be touched with the frustrations and inadequacies of the human condition.

Christ is a priest

   b) in that He received a Divine Appointment to that office. (5:4-6)
   However, Aaron was called of God, but Christ was established with an Oath.

Christ is a priest

   c) in that He is a priest of a new and separate order – 'You are a priest forever in the order of Melchizedek.' (5:6)
   Christ is not a continuation of the Jewish system in any way. However, His functions and ministry may be understood by a comparison with the Jewish system, even though His priesthood issues from an order which is both greater than Aaron, and was established prior to the Jewish system.

What is the Order of Melchizedek?

1. **He was a King and a Priest**
    King of Salem and Priest of God. However, such a combination of Offices was never allowed in the Jewish system.

2. **He Blessed Abraham**

    i)   Scripture says: 'And without question, the person who has the power to give a blessing is greater than the one who is blessed.' (Heb. 7:7) Abraham, the Father of the Jewish system is here designated 'the lesser', and is blessed by 'the greater'.

    ii) Abraham paid tithes to Melchizedek. It must be considered that Levi (the priestly tribe) was yet in the loins of Abraham and there is, in the Hebrew way of thinking, an understanding that the Jewish priests paid tithes through Abraham to Melchizedek, thereby acknowledging the supremacy of Melchizedek!

3. **Melchizedek was like the Son of God** in that he had no known beginning or end; no recorded parents. He suddenly appears on the scene of time, unknown; never to appear again—and without end!

What were the duties of God's High Priest?

THE DIFFERENCES BETWEEN THESE ORDERS	
AARON'S PRIESTHOOD	**CHRIST'S PRIESTHOOD**
Appointed without an Oath	Appointed with an Oath
High Priest over Tribe of Levi and the Tabernacle	High Priest over '*the house of God.*'
	Note: Other references confirm that this phrase 'house' includes both Jews and Gentiles. Christ is the Son over his own house, '*whose house we are, if we hold fast the confidence . . .*' (3:6) '*the household of faith*' (Gal.6:10) Of the '*household of God.*' (Eph.2:19)
Aaron entered the Most Holy Place with a blood sacrifice.	Christ entered into Heaven '*with the sacrifice of himself.*' (Heb. 4:14 & 9:26)
	Note: a) God's presence cannot be contained in a box (Ark of Covenant). The Most Holy Place can only be symbolic of God's dwelling place. God's presence wasn't there when they dismantled the Tabernacle—the Cloud and the Pillar of Fire had already moved on. **b)** God was explicit: The Tent must be an exact replica of what Moses had seen in Heaven. Christ therefore, was found in the actual presence of God, presenting himself on our behalf.
Aaron was the High Priest over his fellow priests, members of his 'family'. These priests offered a) gifts and b) sacrifices in the Outer Courts	The Order of Melchizedek involves US. We also have become priests under our Great High Priest.
	'*Having a High Priest over the house of God, let us draw near . . . and has made us kings and priests to His God and Father.*' (Heb.10:22 & Rev.1:6)

Because of the above differences:

- We may enter into the Holy Place, because our High Priest has abolished the veil which blocks the way into God's presence.

- We don't need to bring a sacrifice for sin because of the 'once for all time' sacrifice of our High Priest, who has made a 'new and living way' for us.

- The heavenly ministry of our High Priest continues forever, 'Now to appear in the presence of God for us!' (Heb 9:24)

- We may come with boldness to 'find grace to help in time of need (4:16)

- It is part of our priestly ministry:

- To offer the sacrifice of praise to God continually, that is the fruit of our lips.

- To do good • To be hospitable (Heb.13:15/16)

- To present our bodies a living sacrifice, which is your 'reasonable service.' (Rom.12:1)

'Reasonable service' means 'your worship offered by mind(reason) and heart(service).'

Chapter 13:

Now for the Other Stuff

Other literary forms in the Scriptures

As much as one-third of the Bible is written in some poetic form or another; so that biblical poetry has been described as the 'Love Language of God' However, the English language—a product of the Western mind-set—often becomes a barrier to understanding the full depth of a scriptural text or passage, when the subtleties of a particular poetic form are lost in translation!

The various forms of poetry in the original Hebrew or Aramaic languages would have been recognized by those early readers, and may well have become a means of easily remembering the teaching of their scriptures.

'Types and Shadows' are therefore only one of several literary forms clearly identified in the Scriptures; and diligent students will be keen to identify numerous other forms as they continues their studies.

The most common of these are briefly covered in this chapter—and the reader is encouraged to further their knowledge by examining books and resources which deal in depth with these and other literary formats.

[1] Understanding Chiasms

The basic idea of a chiasm (pronounced 'ki' as in kite, plus 'asm' as in spasm) is that words, phrases, or other elements can be arranged to mirror each other—so that the text lays out a given set of meanings and then goes back through their parallels in the reverse order. When reading scripture, the reader must remember a basic rule i.e. there is frequently an obvious as well as a hidden meaning to a statement or passage. The use of chiasms is a well-known Hebrew poetic form. However, in a minor form, the concept is not entirely absent from everyday English usage.

The simplest chiasm has the 'AB' format, as follows:

A common saying: **A.** When the **going gets tough**,
     B. the **tough get going**.

An old Nursery Rhyme: **A.** Old **King Cole** was a **merry old soul**
     B. And a **merry old** soul was **he**.

Benjamin Franklin: **A.** By **failing to prepare**,
     B. you are **preparing to fail**.

Jesus: **A.** But many that are **first shall be** last, and the
     B. last shall be first. (Matt.19:30)

However, by far the majority of chiasms will have an 'ABXBA' (or longer) format as in Isaiah 55:8/9:

A. For My thoughts are not your thoughts,

    B. Nor are your ways My ways, says the Lord,

        X. For as the heavens are higher than the earth

    B. So are My ways higher than your ways,

A. And My thoughts than your thoughts.' (Isa.55:8/9)

It has been said that studying chiasms is like looking for the 'meat in the sandwich', because the central element of the chiasm (the 'X'), functions as the focal point of the entire statement. It is the tipping point of the verse or passage, and must be given due significance. Notice this tipping point in the story of the Prodigal Son (Luke 15:11-31)

A. The father had two sons

  B. the younger brother journeys to a far country

    C. the younger brother began to be in want

      X. and when he came to himself … 'I have sinned'

    C. (the older brother) You have never given me a goat

  B. I have never transgressed your commandment

A. Son, you are always with me … your brother … is alive again

Notice it again in Joel 3:17-21

A. God dwells in Zion (17a)

  B. Jerusalem is holy (17b)

    C. Foreign invaders are banished (17c)

      X. The blessings of the Kingdom (18)

    C. Foreign enemies are destroyed (19)

  B. Jerusalem and Judah are preserved (20–21a)

A. God dwells in Zion (21b)

The chiasm in Matthew 6:24 (from the Sermon on the Mount) **is a little different in that it has two 'X' points.** This passage is often presented as if we have a choice about which Master we ***serve***—but when we let the 'X' become the guiding truth, the passage becomes more about our attitude (***love and loyalty***), then about which Master. It is suggesting that **it is possible for a person to serve God without really loving Him**!

A. No one can serve two masters;

    B. For either he will hate the one

        X. and love the other

        X. or else he will be loyal to one

    B. and despise the other.

A. You cannot serve God and mammon(wealth)

Isaiah 1:21-26 is a longer passage and has more points:

A. The faithful city has become a harlot!

    B. It is full of injustice;

        C. Your silver has become dross,

            D. (There is no justice in the land - vs.23)

            X. Therefore says …The Mighty One of Israel …

            D. I will rid Myself of My adversaries, and take vengeance on My enemies.

        C. (I will) thoroughly purge away your dross … and take away all your alloy.

    B. I will restore your judges as at the first,

A. You shall be called the city of righteousness, the faithful city.

And take a look at Joshua 1:5–9 :

A. I will not leave you nor forsake you.

    B. Be strong and of good courage

        C. Observe to do according to all the law

          … that you may prosper wherever you go.

          X. You shall meditate in (*the law*) day and night

        C. Observe to do according to all that is written

            … then you will have good success.

    B. Be strong and of good courage;

A. for the Lord your God *is* with you wherever you go."

And lastly, take a look at Romans 10:9/10 – considered to be a basic Salvation statement:

'the word of faith which we preach ...

A. That if you confess with your mouth the Lord Jesus

> **B**. And believe in your heart that God has raised Him from the dead

> > **X. You will be saved.**

> **B**. For with the heart one believes unto righteousness,

A. And with the mouth confession is made unto salvation.'

The Scriptures are full of chiasms. Have fun finding them – and always pay particular attention to the 'X' factor!

[2] Understanding Parallelisms

In English poetry, one of the tools used is 'end rhyme'— as in the Nursery Rhyme:

> 'Jack and Jill went up the hill to fetch a pail of ***water***
>
> Jack fell ***down*** and broke his ***crown***
>
> and Jill came tumbling ***after***.'

In English poetry this 'end rhyme' is therefore formed by matching ***sounds***. However, in contrast, a parallelism is formed by matching ***thoughts***.

A good example of a parallelism is located in Psalm 119:105:

'Your Word is a (**A**) lamp to my (**B**) feet

> > - And a (**A**) light to my (**B**) path.'

This scripture teaches us, for example, that the Word of God is like a focused lamp or torch, as well as a light that covers a larger area—and, that the Word not only shows me the path to follow, but how to place my feet on that path.

At other times a parallelism will not repeat or reverse, as in a chiasm. Rather, **it amplifies and re-states the phrase in such a way that it adds to the meaning of the first phrase**, so that, to quote Aristotle: 'the whole is greater than the sum of its parts' — **as in Proverbs 17:25** :

'A foolish son is a **grief** to his **father** and **bitterness** to **her who bore him**.'

This parallelism makes the obvious point that foolish children are a disappointment to their parents; but makes the added observation that fathers and mothers each feel a unique pain in having a foolish child. (See also Proverbs 10:1)

Always pay attention to both the sameness and uniqueness of the parallel words used in Parallelisms.

Parallelisms are frequently found in Psalms and Proverbs, as well as in other areas of the Bible, as follows:

Matthew 6:13 : 'And do not lead us into temptation, But deliver us from the evil one.'

Psalm 1:6 : 'For the Lord knows the way of the righteous, but the way of the ungodly shall perish.'

II Timothy 2:11-13 :
    'This is a faithful saying:
    For if we died with Him — We shall also live with Him
    If we endure — We shall also reign with Him
    If we deny Him — He also will deny us.
    If we are faithless - He remains faithful; He cannot deny Himself.'

Psalm 120:2 : 'Save me, O Lord, from lying lips and from deceitful tongues.'

The idea of 'lying lips' in the first line of the poetry is repeated in the second line as 'deceitful tongues.' The two expressions use different words to describe the same thing—a mouth that can't tell the truth. The meanings of both lines are synonymous.

Proverbs 3:11 : 'My son, do not despise the Lord's discipline and do not resent his rebuke.'

Isaiah 53:5 : 'But he was pierced for our transgressions, he was crushed for our iniquities.'

There are hundreds to be found. Now I have told you about them, you will find them everywhere!

There is a Significant Parallelism between Joseph and King David

In the New Testament Jesus is often referred to as 'The Son of David'—as when the blind man called out: 'Jesus, Son of David, have mercy on me' (Luke 18:38). However, it is not so well known that early Jewish Rabbis also referred to the Messiah as 'Messiah, Son of Joseph.'

They well understood the literary parallelism between the lives of Joseph and King David; and they believed their coming Messiah would, in some way, mirror events in the life of Joseph.

Watch this parallelism between Joseph (Genesis 37-50) and David (I Samuel 16-20) unfold, in the following ways:

Joseph was 17 years of age when he received important dreams
David was the youngest son when anointed by Samuel

Both Joseph and David care for sheep
Both are sent to seek the welfare of their brothers

Joseph's brothers hated him
David's brothers despised him

Joseph and David's rulers i.e. Pharoah and King Saul, both recognise that God is with them

Both were married by a King to non-Jewish women
Both were aged 30 when receiving positions of honour

Both men are considered to be handsome

Joseph resisted the temptation of a married woman – but sadly David did not

Now watch as the life of JESUS mirrors that of JOSEPH

• Both are despised   • Aged thirty is a key time for both men
• Both stripped of their clothing   • Both became servants
• Both resisted temptation   • Both falsely accused
• Both described as shepherds   • Both accused of being a dreamer
• Both were targeted for death by their enemies
• Both sold for silver coins   • Both counted among criminals
• Both gave hope to a criminal   • Both were given-up as dead
• Both their stories end with being reconciled with their brothers
• Both are welcomed among Gentiles and become great leaders

[3] Understanding Inclusion, Bracketing and the Envelope Structure

'Inclusion' or 'Inclusio' is another literary form, sometimes known as 'bracketing' or the 'envelope structure'. It is not always well-understood. This is a device used to put a framework around, not just a sentence, but usually a larger amount of text. As a picture-frame will draw your eyes toward the picture, so 'inclusio' is a framework which draws the bible student's attention to the significance of the material within the framework.

In some ways this 'envelope structure' can also be seen as an extended Chiasm, in which the first and last statements could be seen as representing 'AA' and the middle material making the Chiasm reference of 'A--X--A'.

There is an easy-to-see example in the story of Jesus and the fig tree in Mark 11:12-25. The 'framework' of this passage is the rebuke of the fig tree in vss. 12-14 (for having leaves but no fruit)—and the observation of the dead tree the next morning in vss.20/21. In between these two time periods Jesus had observed the fruitlessness of the Temple (and its proceedings), in that it demonstrated performance over substance. Jesus then declared God's frustration, if not anger, at this situation, in much the same way as He had judged the fig tree.

Some Other Well-Accepted Examples:

In Ruth (1:1) we are told that Elimelech leaves Bethlehem for Moab – and in (1:22) we are told Ruth and Naomi leave Moab for Bethlehem. Like the opening scene of a theatrical performance, the details of Ruth chapter one set the scene for the remainder of the story.

Psalm 46:1 reads: 'God is our refuge and strength, A very present help in trouble' and the last verse reads: 'The Lord of hosts is with us; The God of Jacob is our refuge.' This is a valid framework, even though the words are reversed—somewhat like a Parallelism.

In Psalm 118 the first and last verses read: 'Oh, give thanks to the Lord, for He is good! For His mercy endures forever.'

In Matthew's Gospel there are several Inclusions:

1. The famous Sermon on the Mount (Matt.5:3-10) begins and ends with the phrase: '... theirs is the kingdom of heaven.'

2. After the above introduction the Sermon on the Mount is further framed with a reference to the 'Law and the Prophets' in Matthew 5:17 and 7:12.

3. Matthew's report of the first part of Jesus' Ministry is neatly framed by an account on his teaching and his miracles.

> It begins: 'And Jesus went about all Galilee, teaching in their synagogues, preaching the gospel of the kingdom, and healing all kinds of sickness and all kinds of disease among the people' (Matt.4:23)

> — and concludes: 'Then Jesus went about all the cities and villages, teaching in their synagogues, preaching the gospel of the kingdom, and healing every sickness and every disease among the people.' (Matt.9:35)

These two verses 'frame' the five chapters between, which present some very typical teachings and miracles of Jesus as He demonstrates both the ways of the Kingdom and the power of the Kingdom of God.

The book of Hebrews contains two significant quotes from the prophet Jeremiah i.e. Chapters 8:8-10 and 10:16-18. These two quotes are considered to be an 'inclusio', within which the writer to Hebrews deals with the most important subject of the Priesthood of Jesus Christ for all believers.

Mark's Gospel presents us with a significant 'inclusio': A blind man is healed at Bethsaida in Mark 8:22-26, and a second blind man is healed at Jericho in Mark 10:46-52.

These two incidents 'frame' a period of time in which Jesus predicted His death and sufferings on three separate occasions: The first begins at Mark 8:31; the second begins at Mark 9:30, and the third occasion begins at Mark 10:32.

Each of these predictions cause some kind of unbelief/confused reaction by Jesus' disciples; together with discussions about who is to be the greatest among them in some future kingdom!

In their lack of understanding of God's true purposes in Christ these disciples are as blind as the blind men—and need healing … with the first blind man requiring Jesus to lay hands on him twice, before he was healed!

Note to Bible students: Don't forget to keep your own listing of any other 'inclusions' you discover as you read through the scriptures and/or find when reading bible study books.

[4] Understanding Psalms which are Written as Acrostics
– using the twenty-two letters of the Hebrew Alphabet:

[**Note**: The beauty and skill of the use of the Acrostic form is lost when translated into English]

Psalm 119 has no stated author, but the complexity of its construction suggests King David.
- This Psalm has twenty-two sections
- Each section has eight lines
- Every line in a section begins with the same Hebrew letter
- Each section employs eight different terms to describe/define the *Word of God* i.e. commandment, testimonies, precepts, ways, law, judgments, statutes etc.

Psalms 9 & 10 were once a single Psalm – written as an Acrostic psalm by King David.

Refer also: Psalms 25 – 34 – 37 – 111 and 145.

Proverbs 31:10-31 – The Noble Wife: is written as an Acrostic section.

[**Note**: These verses are often used to extoll the virtues of womanhood. However, from another perspective they are a poetic and prophetic description of the Church—the Bride of Christ!

Read this passage for yourself and see what I mean.

[5] Understanding Similes, Metaphors, Comparisons or Implications etc: ('like' or 'as')

Dozens of differing literary devices have been identified by literary experts, in languages all over the world.

However, they are all essentially poetic forms of writing which compare one thing to another thing. Such comparisons assist us to visualise a truth, as well as imparting a deeper level of meaning to the words used.

Here are a few examples from the many thousands to be found throughout Scripture. Take some time to visualise the *'one thing'* and the *'other thing'* contained in these statements, and then notice how your understanding of the meaning of the whole statement is enlarged and strengthened:

Ps. 1:3 'He shall be ***like a tree*** planted by the rivers of water, that brings forth its fruit in its season.'

Ps. 84:11 (NLT) 'For the Lord God ***is a sun and shield***; the Lord will give grace and glory (or: favour and honour).'

Ps. 22:16 'My enemies surround me ***like a pack of dogs***; an evil gang closes in on me.'

I Thessalonians 5:2 '… the day of the Lord so comes ***as a thief*** in the night.'

Matthew 13:44 'The kingdom of heaven is ***like treasure hidden in a field***, which a man found and hid; and for joy over it he goes and sells all that he had and buys that field.'

Matthew 28:3 '… His appearance was ***like lightning*** and his clothing ***as white as snow.***'

Matthew 23:27 '… you are *like white-washed tombs* which indeed appear beautiful outwardly, but inside are full of dead men's bones and all uncleanness.'

Matthew 13:52 '… *a disciple in the kingdom of heaven is like a homeowner* who brings from his storeroom new gems of truth as well as old.'

Proverbs 10:26 '*Like vinegar to the teeth and smoke to the eyes*, so is the lazy one to those who send him.'

Proverbs 25:11 'A word fitly spoken i*s like apples of gold in pictures of silver.*'

Matthew 10:16 'Behold, I send you forth *as sheep in the midst of wolves*: be ye therefore *wise as serpents*, and *harmless as doves.*'

(6) Understanding Metaphors

Many of the above examples also contain metaphors. Jesus frequently used metaphors in the course of His ministry—metaphors like: sheep, shepherds, sowers, wheat seed, tares, harvest, bread, pearls, trees, vines, landowners and talents etc. You know immediately that these words are intended to convey something greater than the actual item named. For instance, trees are used to depict people, and animals or other inanimate objects are also used to depict people, nations and churches, etc.

(7) Understanding Personification

A classic example of the use of personification is in the book of Proverbs, where wisdom—or a lack thereof—is described as either a Wise Woman or a Prostitute.

There are so many examples of personifications. For instance: A *lamb is not really an animal*, it represents the sacrificial lamb, Jesus Christ. The candlesticks in Revelation 2 & 3 are really the seven churches; the stars personify the leaders of those churches.

Frequently **snakes and serpents = Satan**, as in Revelation 20:2 'He laid hold of the dragon, **that serpent of old**, who is the Devil and Satan, and bound him for a thousand years.'

For instance, **hail = God's word** that sweeps away lies, as in: Isaiah 28:17: 'Also I will make justice the measuring line, and righteousness the plummet; **the hail will sweep away the refuge of lies**, and the waters will overflow the hiding place.'

(Refer under (8) below for other examples of Personifications found in the book of Proverbs.)

[8] Understanding Hyperbole or Exaggeration

Hyperbole is another literary device, where exaggeration is used, often with great effect. When studying the Scriptures, save yourself a lot of trouble by not taking literally what is meant as hyperbole!

As with similes, metaphors and other literary devices, it pays to meditate on hyperbole whenever you encounter it.

Here are some classic examples of hyperbole:

Ps. 6:6
'All night I make my bed swim; I drench my couch with my tears.'

That's an awful lot of tears!

Matthew 5:29
'If your right eye causes you to sin, pluck it out and cast it from you ...'

Both I and Jesus, would be horrified if you did this literally! But you must eliminate anything which causes you to stumble in life.

Luke 10:4
'Carry neither money bag, knapsack, nor sandals; and **greet no one along the road**.'

This sounds rude, until you recognize that in Jewish culture a 'hello' along the road could even involve you in an overnight stay, if you acknowledged it. Don't get distracted from your purpose!

Luke 9:25

What profit is it to a man if gains the whole world, and is himself destroyed or lost?'

No one can ever own the whole world! This is pure hyperbole—so, work out the meaning for yourself.

11 Chronicles 1:15

'Also the king made silver and gold as common in Jerusalem as stones, and he made cedars as abundant as the sycamores which are in the lowland.'

This is a hyperbolic statement to let you know that King Solomon was unbelievably rich!

John 12:19

'The Pharisees therefore said among themselves, "You see that you are accomplishing nothing. Look, the world has gone after Him!"'

Don't let envy or jealously cloud your thinking. Many people did follow Jesus – but there were still many who were confused and antagonistic. A simple crowd does not constitute the whole world!

Let me conclude this section by encouraging you to look out for instances where body-parts are ascribed to God, as in:

Ps. 31:2

'Bow down Your *ear* to me, deliver me speedily …'

Ps. 17:8

'Keep me as the ***apple of Your eye***; Hide me under the shadow of Your ***wings*** …'

And those occasions where human characteristics are given to inanimate objects, such as:

Ps. 35:10
'All my bones shall **say**, Lord, who is like You ...'

[9] Understanding Proverbs – as in the Book of Proverbs:

You need to remember the term: 'First the natural – then the spiritual' as you read the book of Proverbs and study the references to the many characters in the book. Look for the spiritual truths, as well as the practical instruction found in statements about the following persons:

The Young Man's Mother - Represents reverence and respect

The Young Man's Wife - Represents righteousness, and wholesomeness

The Prostitute - Represents all unrighteousness and immoral ways

The Woman (Wisdom) - Represents all righteousness and moral ways

The Cranky Wife - Represents the bitter person (Also refer: Prov. 21:9, 21:19 and 27:15)

The Young Man's Father - Represents respect, experience

The Young Man himself - Represents YOU – and your standing before God!

The Ungodly Man - Represents all forms of spiritual foolishness

The Rebel (Foolish man) - Represents the person who doesn't listen to Wisdom

The Lazy Man - Represents the spiritually lazy person

| **The Drunk** | - Represents a lack of discipline in all areas of life |
| **The King** | - Represents holders of authority at all levels of society and life |

The Sayings of Agur
Proverbs 30:15-31 (Three-and four-line sayings)

These five unusual sayings of Agur all have a common opening line i.e. 'There are three things ... no four ...'. This way of speaking draws your attention to the last line, which is, in fact, the most important line in the Proverb.

Proverbs 30:15/16 – Four things never satisfied
                    'And the fire never says, 'Enough!'

Proverbs 30:18/19 – Four Wonderful things
                    'And the way of a man with a virgin.'

Proverbs 30:21/23 – Four things the earth despises
                    'And a maidservant who succeeds her mistress.'

Proverbs 30:24/28 – Four things both wise and small
                    'the spider/lizard ... is in kings' palaces.'

Proverbs 30:29/31 – Four majestic beings
                    'a king whose troops are with him.'

The Sayings of King Lemuel – Proverbs 31

'King Lemuel' was the pet-name given to King Solomon by his mother.

The Tabernacle and it's Materials

The Sequence in which God gave Instructions for the construction of the Tabernacle and its furnishings. Note how, after gathering the required materials, this listing commences from the central item—the Ark of the Covenant—working, mostly outwards, to the least of the items:

ITEM:	EXODUS REFERENCE
Materials required	25:1-9
Ark of the Covenant	25:10-16
Mercy Seat	25:17-22
Table of Shewbread	25:23-30
Golden Candlestick	25:31-40
Linen Curtains (for Inner Tabernacle)	26:1-6
Tent Covering of Goats Hair	26:7-13
Tent Covering of Rams Skins dyed red	26:14
Tent Covering of Badgers Skins	26:14

Appendix B

Parables of the Old Testament

Trees making themselves a King	- Judges 9
Samson's Riddle	- Judges 14
Poor Man's Lamb (Nathan to David)	- 11 Samuel 12
Woman of Tekoa & her two sons	- 11 Sam 14
Escape Prisoner – addressed to Ahab	- 1 Kings 20
Vision of Micaiah (told by Ahab)	- 1 Kings 22
Thistle and Cedar (told to Amaziah))	- 11 Kings 14
Drunkard (Counsel from Solomon)	- Proverbs 23
Sluggard to his Vineyard (to Israel)	- Proverbs 24
Poor Wise Man (Counsel from Solomon)	- Ecclesiastes 9
Unfruitful Vineyard (to Israel)	- Isaiah 5
The Plow Man	- Isaiah 28
The Linen Waist Cloth	- Jeremiah 13
Potter & the Clay	- Jeremiah 18
Great Eagle and the Vine	- Ezekiel 17
The Lion's Whelps	- Ezekiel 19
Two Harlots	- Ezekiel 23
The Boiling Pot and its Scum	- Ezekiel 24
The Cedar of Lebanon	- Ezekiel 31
The Sea Monster	- Ezekiel 32

Note: The Prophet Ezekiel performed a number of interesting 'Enacted Parables' about Jerusalem's Siege, Iniquity, Confinement, Starvation and Sinfulness, as described in Ezekiel chapters 4 and 5.

Parables of the New Testament

Listed below are some of the most prominent parables of Jesus in the New Testament—drawn from the Gospels of Matthew, Mark and Luke. Jesus always used parables to speak to the crowds which followed Him, but He never spoke in parables to the disciples (except to explain, in private, something they may not have understood).

Because John's Gospel concentrates on the seven 'miraculous signs' of Jesus (John 2:11), there is very little recorded of His public discourses. However, there are a few occasions when Jesus speaks to His disciples in parabolic terms i.e.

The Coming Harvest	- John 4
I am the Bread of Life	- John 6
I am the Good Shepherd	- John 10
I am the Vine you are the Branches	- John 15

OTHER PROMINENT NEW TESTAMENT PARABLES

Sower	- Matt.13	- Mark 4	- Luke 8
Wheat and Tares	- Matt.13		
Mustard Seed	- Matt.13	- Mark 4	

Seed planted in the ground		- Mark 4	
Leaven	- Matt.13		
Concealed Treasure	- Matt.13		
Pearl of Great Price	- Matt.13		
Casting Net into Sea	- Matt.13		
Two Debtors			- Luke 7
Unforgiving Servant	- Matt.18		
Good Samaritan			- Luke 10
Friend at Midnight			- Luke 11
Rich Fool			- Luke 12
Wedding Feast			- Luke 12
Fig Tree			- Luke 13
Great Supper			- Luke 14
Lost Sheep, Coin & Prodigal Son			- Luke 15
Unjust Steward			- Luke 16
Rich Man and Lazarus			- Luke 16
Unjust Judge			- Luke 18
Pharisee and Publican			- Luke 18
Labourers in Vineyard	- Matt. 20		
Pounds			- Luke 19
Two Sons	- Matt. 21		
Tenants	- Matt. 21	- Mark 12	- Luke 20
Marriage Feast	- Matt. 22		
Wise/Foolish Virgins	- Matt. 25		
Talent to Servants	- Matt. 25		
Sheep & Goats	- Matt. 25		

Appendix D

Types used in the Book of Hebrews

The New Testament book of Hebrews is full of instances where the writer refers to people and incidents in the Old Testament which point to Christ:

MOSES is typical of Christ (3:1-6)

JOSHUA's entry into the **Promised Land** is typical of Christ giving spiritual 'rest' and fulfilment to His people (4:8-10), together with the whole concept of the **Sabbath** also being a type of the above described 'rest'.

MELCHIZEDEK is spoken of extensively as a type of the priestly role of Jesus Christ in Hebrews chapters 5-7; as is the **Aaronic** priesthood contrasted with Christ's role. At one point the writer leaves us in suspense, with the sad comment: '... Melchizedek, of whom we have much to say, and hard to explain, since you have become dull of hearing.' (Hebrew 5:10/11)

The **Work of the Priests** in the Tabernacle is a type of the Ministry of Christ—and the **Tabernacle Furnishings** are also considered to be types of Christ (although the writer leaves us in suspense at 9:5 '... Of these things we cannot now speak in detail.') Also refer chapter 9:23-23:

'This is why the Tabernacle and everything in it, which were copies of things in heaven, had to be purified by the blood of animals. But the real things in heaven had to be purified with far better sacrifices than the blood of animals. For Christ did not enter into a holy place made with human hands, which was only a copy of the true one in heaven. He entered into heaven itself to appear now before God on our behalf ...' (Hebrews 9:23-24 NLT)

Chapter Nine also speaks of the various, and imperfect, Sacrifices associated with the Tabernacle, which are also contrasted with the perfect and all-inclusive sacrifice of Christ.

Abel's Blood is contrasted with the Blood of Jesus: 'the blood of Jesus speaks better things than that of Abel' (Heb. 11:4; 12:24). Abel's blood cries out for vengeance, but Christ's blood cries out for mercy ...

'You have come to Jesus, the one who mediates the new covenant between God and people, and to the sprinkled blood, which speaks of forgiveness instead of crying out for vengeance like the blood of Abel.' (Hebrews 12:24 NLT)

Hebrews Chapter Eleven: All the many persons named in this chapter lived their lives by faith in the Promises of God. However, many of the circumstances of their lives are implicit types of Christ—worthy of a student's further study!

The giving of the Law on **Mount Sinai**—and its terrible scene and serious consequences is strongly contrasted with the great 'Mount Zion and to the city of the living God, the heavenly Jerusalem ...' (12:18-24)

To help you test your understanding of the subject of 'types and shadows' here's some suggested Homework topics for you to consider:

Write an Essay: (at least 300 words) entitled: 'Understanding Calvary Through Types & Shadows.'

Write an Essay: (at least 300 words) entitled:
'How the work of the Tabernacle priests depicts the earthly ministry of Jesus, and also His current heavenly ministry.'

Write an Essay: (No less than 300 words) entitled: 'The Menorah – its Base, Shaft and Branches.' However, before doing this be sure to thoroughly read the section on the Menorah in chapter 8 – and associate this with what you read in Exodus 25:31-40, together with scripture references like: 'God was in Christ reconciling the world unto Himself . . .' (2 Corinthians 5:19) and 'I am the true vine … you are the branches … my Father is the husbandman …' i.e. owner, life-giver to the Vineyard etc. (John 15:1-8)

Write an Essay: (no less than 300words) entitled: 'The Day the Veil was Torn in Two.' In this Essay you will demonstrate your understanding of Matthew 27:50-51 – 'And Jesus cried out again with a loud voice, and yielded up His spirit. Then, behold, the veil of the temple was torn in two from top to bottom; …'

[i] 'The LOST Kingdom – Gateway to your Inheritance' by Adrian Beale. Refer www.everrestministries.com

[ii] The Mystic Awakening by Adrian Beale, published by Destiny Image Publishers Inc. Shippensburg PA USA.

[iii] Refer: Bobsorge.com for a collection of many other similarities.

[iv] Henry M. Morris, Ph.D. 2003. The "I Am's" Of Christ. Acts & Facts. 32 (4). Morris was a co-founder of the Creation Research Society.

About the Author

Frank is a graduate of the International Bible Training Institute (IBTI) at Burgess Hill, Sussex, England—and has been preaching and teaching the Word of God since his teens.

Together with Eunice his wife, he has pastored several churches in Australia—as well as teaching at Bible Schools in Australia and in the nearby Pacific Islands region.

As well as serving for many years as Overseas Missions Director for the International Church of the Foursquare Gospel (Australia) for its missionary enterprise in Papua New Guinea, Frank has always worked to see the balance between the teaching of the sound Word of God and a strong demonstration of the Holy Spirit's power and presence.

www.ingramcontent.com/pod-product-compliance
Lightning Source LLC
Chambersburg PA
CBHW071551040426

42452CB00008B/1133

9 781734 499919